Lecture Notes in Computer Science 12339

More information about this subseries at http://www.springer.com/series/7407

Katrin Amunts · Lucio Grandinetti ·
Thomas Lippert · Nicolai Petkov (Eds.)

Brain-Inspired Computing

4th International Workshop, BrainComp 2019
Cetraro, Italy, July 15–19, 2019
Revised Selected Papers

 Springer

Editors
Katrin Amunts
Forschungszentrum Jülich
Jülich, Germany

C. und O. Vogt-Institut für Hirnforschung
Universitätsklinikum
Düsseldorf, Germany

Thomas Lippert
Forschungszentrum Jülich
Jülich, Germany

Goethe-Universität Frankfurt
Frankfurt am Main, Germany

Lucio Grandinetti
DIMES
University of Calabria
Arcavacada di Rende, Italy

Nicolai Petkov
University of Groningen
Groningen, Groningen, The Netherlands

ISSN 0302-9743   ISSN 1611-3349 (electronic)
Lecture Notes in Computer Science
ISBN 978-3-030-82426-6   ISBN 978-3-030-82427-3 (eBook)
https://doi.org/10.1007/978-3-030-82427-3

LNCS Sublibrary: SL1 – Theoretical Computer Science and General Issues

This Springer imprint is published by the registered company Springer Nature Switzerland AG
The registered company address is: Gewerbestrasse 11, 6330 Cham, Switzerland

Preface

Together neuroscience and computing are driving forces for research and innovation. They enable new insights into the brain's complexity as well as biological information processing and lay ground for progress in future computing. Making use of this collaborative effort by bringing together relevant key players in the field of neuroscience and future computing, the workshop on Brain-Inspired Computing (BrainComp) aims to shed a light on the digital transformation of neuroscience by high performance computing (HPC).

The International Workshop on Brain-Inspired Computing, held in Cetraro, Italy, during July 15–19, 2019, was jointly organized by the Human Brain Project, the University of Calabria, the University of Groningen, and the Research Centre Juelich. A highlight of this workshop edition was the BrainComp Young Researchers Competition in which young researchers were invited to solve neuroscientific problems by using HPC resources that were kindly provided by leading European HPC centers. The workshop proceedings include contributions from renowned scientists and early career researchers who participated in the workshop. It includes research on brain atlasing, multi-scale models and simulation, and HPC as well as data infrastructures for neuroscience, as well as artificial and natural neural architectures. All submissions were evaluated in a single-blind review process. The acceptance rate for BrainComp 2019 was 100%.

July 2021

Katrin Amunts
Lucio Grandinetti
Thomas Lippert
Nicolai Petkov

Organization

Program and Organization Committee

Katrin Amunts   Research Center Juelich, Germany
Lucio Grandinetti   University of Calabria, Italy
Thomas Lippert   Research Center Juelich, Germany
Nicolai Petkov   University of Groningen, The Netherlands

Review Committee

Katrin Amunts   Research Center Juelich, Germany
Paolo Carloni   Research Center Juelich, Germany
Pier Stanislao Paolucci National Institute for National Physics, Italy
Nicolai Petkov   University of Groningen, The Netherlands

Sponsors

CRAY
Mellanox Technologies
NVIDIA
ParTec Cluster Competence Center
Research Center Juelich
University of Calabria
University of Groningen
University of Salento
The Human Brain Project

Acknowledgement

This conference proceedings received funding from the European Union's Horizon 2020 Research and Innovation Programme, grant agreement and 945539 (HBP SGA3).

Contents

Machine Learning and Deep Learning Approaches in Human Brain Mapping

A High-Resolution Model of the Human Entorhinal Cortex in the 'BigBrain' – Use Case for Machine Learning and 3D Analyses

Sabrina Behuet[1]([✉]), Sebastian Bludau[1], Olga Kedo[1], Christian Schiffer[1,2], Timo Dickscheid[1,2], Andrea Brandstetter[1], Philippe Massicotte[3], Mona Omidyeganeh[3,4], Alan Evans[4], and Katrin Amunts[1,5]

[1] Institute of Neuroscience and Medicine (INM-1), Research Centre Jülich, Jülich, Germany
s.behuet@fz-juelich.de
[2] Helmholtz AI, Research Centre Jülich, Jülich, Germany
[3] National Research Council of Canada (NRC), Ottawa, Canada
[4] Department of Neurology and Neurosurgery, Montréal Neurological Institute (MNI), McGill University, Montréal, Canada
[5] C. and O. Vogt Institute of Brain Research, Medical Faculty, Heinrich-Heine University, Düsseldorf, Germany

Abstract. The 'BigBrain' is a high-resolution data set of the human brain that enables three-dimensional (3D) analyses with a 20 μm spatial resolution at nearly cellular level. We use this data set to explore pre-α (cell) islands of layer 2 in the entorhinal cortex (EC), which are early affected in Alzheimer's disease and have therefore been the focus of research for many years. They appear mostly in a round and elongated shape as shown in microscopic studies. Some studies suggested that islands may be interconnected based on analyses of their shape and size in two-dimensional (2D) space. Here, we characterized morphological features (shape, size, and distribution) of pre-α islands in the 'BigBrain', based on 3D-reconstructions of gapless series of cell-body-stained sections. The EC was annotated manually, and a machine-learning tool was trained to identify and segment islands with subsequent visualization using high-performance computing (HPC). Islands were visualized as 3D surfaces and their geometry was analyzed. Their morphology was complex: they appeared to be composed of interconnected islands of different types found in 2D histological sections of EC, with various shapes in 3D. Differences in the rostral-to-caudal part of EC were identified by specific distribution and size of islands, with implications for connectivity and function of the EC. 3D compactness analysis found more round and complex islands than elongated ones. The present study represents a use case for studying large microscopic data sets. It provides reference data for studies, e.g. investigating neurodegenerative diseases, where specific alterations in layer 2 were previously reported.

Keywords: Entorhinal cortex · Pre-α islands · 'BigBrain' · Machine-learning · 3D visualization · Large data sets

© The Author(s) 2021
K. Amunts et al. (Eds.): BrainComp 2019, LNCS 12339, pp. 3–21, 2021.
https://doi.org/10.1007/978-3-030-82427-3_1

1 Introduction

The 'BigBrain' model represents a three-dimensional (3D)-reconstructed data set at histological sections with a spatial resolution of 20 μm isotropic [1]. It is based on a series of 7404 images of histological sections, where each was scanned originally with an in-plane resolution of 10 μm, down-sampled to 20 μm, resulting in a total data size of 1 TByte [1]. This data set and model represents a unique high-resolution anatomical reference for applications from neuroimaging, modeling and simulation, neurophysiology as well as for research on artificial neuronal networks (for an overview of recent research see https://bigbrainproject.org/hiball.html). At the same time, the 'BigBrain' is both a research target and a tool to set up workflows for analyzing large data sets, where methods from artificial intelligence (AI), e.g. machine learning, are part of advanced workflows running on the supercomputers to advance our understanding of the complexity of the brain. Along this line of reasoning, we here address the microstructural organization of the human **entorhinal cortex (EC)**.

The EC is a brain area of the mesial temporal cortex and occupies the rostral part of the parahippocampal gyrus (PhG) (Fig. 1). A unique feature of this part of the so-called periallocortex is the Substratum dissecans, an almost cell-free sublayer [2–6]. It extends parallel to the cortical surface in the midst of the cortex, macroscopically often separating EC into an inner and an outer principal layer [3, 5]. The most prominent feature of EC is layer 2 (or Stratum stellare [4]), which is composed of neurons clustered into groups with different numbers of neurons and different shapes and sizes, the so-called **pre-α islands** [3, 5] (Fig. 1). The surrounding tissue ('neuropil') separates the pre-α islands from each other. Their morphology can presently only be studied in two-dimensional (2D) histological sections of postmortem brain with a spatial resolution that is much higher than that of magnetic resonance imaging (MRI).

Based on histological studies, the shape of pre-α islands was described as elongated in the rostral and medial part of EC, and round in the caudal extent [2]. This variability of pre-α islands in layer 2 combined with the specific cytoarchitectonic features of other layers along the extent of EC led to a partition of this brain area into several subareas [2, 7, 8]. For example, Brodmann (1909) [7] identified areas (BA)28a and BA28b, while Braak and Braak (1992) [8] defined a medial, lateral, and central subarea.

Layer 2 and its pre-α islands are involved in the so-called perforant pathway that supports the processing of spatial memory and context information [9]. Significant decrease of its pre-α cells [10] among other alterations are found in the early stages of Alzheimer's disease (AD) and may underline early symptoms such as mild cognitive deficits and spatial disorientation. This makes them an interesting research target for the research of AD, but also other neurodegenerative and psychiatric diseases (e.g. Parkinson's disease, schizophrenia) [8, 11].

Previous studies indicated a rather complex morphology of pre-α islands as these islands were connected by "bridges" in different types of sections [8, 12] and section planes [13]. For example, the latter study noted immunolabeled "bridges" in the interstices (spaces between two cell islands) that appeared to connect two islands. However, these morphological analyses were limited to only one section plane (e.g. by using either flat, tangential, or sagittal sections) and were therefore not able to follow the progression of pre-α islands in the other planes to fully characterize their shape and size.

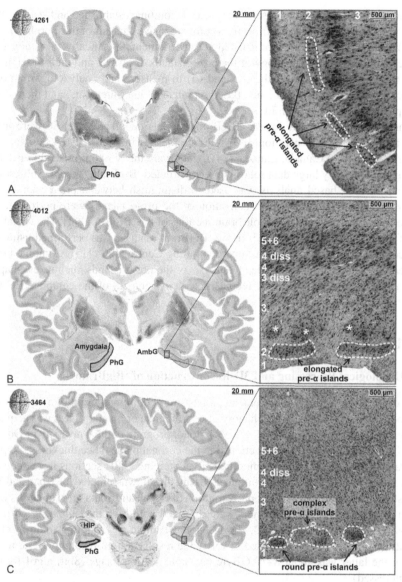

Fig. 1. Coronal sections of the human 'BigBrain' model (20 µm isotropic resolution) of the EC (on the left) and its cytoarchitecture (1 µm in-plane resolution) in its rostral (**A**), intermediate (**B**), and caudal part (**C**) (on the right). Dark contours: EC in the left hemisphere, light contour: right EC. Note the different types of pre-α islands (elongated, round, and complex) in layer 2 (white dotted lines). Section numbers and position in the 'BigBrain' are shown in the upper left corner. Layers of the EC indicated by Arabic numerals. Abbreviations: *AmbG*, Ambient gyrus; *PhG*, Parahippocampal gyrus; *HIP*, Hippocampus. Layers of EC [4]: *1*, Layer 1 (Stratum moleculare); *2*, Layer 2 (Stratum stellare); *3*, Layer 3 (Stratum pyramidale); *3 diss* and *4 diss*, Substrata dissecantia; *4*, Layer 4 (Stratum magnocellulare); *5*, Layer 5 (Stratum parvocellulare); *6*, Layer 6 (Stratum multiforme). * in B: clusters of the superficial layer 3.

Therefore, the aim of the present study was to combine established and state-of-the-art data sets and tools into a workflow for a comprehensive analysis of the morphology of layer 2 pre-α islands in their reconstructed 3D environment. Specifically, this study aims (i) to characterize the morphology of the pre-α islands of layer 2 and their distribution along the longitudinal axis of the EC, and (ii) to measure and analyze distributional features of pre-α islands ('gradients' based on intensity measurements) and their shape ('compactness') in the human EC.

Based on the high-resolution 3D 'BigBrain' model, the left and right EC were annotated, followed by the generation of 3D surface meshes in Atelier3D (A3D, National Research Council of Canada, Canada, [14]), a software that was optimized to visualize and annotate the very large data set of the reconstructed 'BigBrain' model. Subsequent machine-learning based analysis was used to distinguish between pre-α islands and background. Data analysis and visualization of the pre-α islands were performed on cropped annotated parts of the whole brain sections of the 'BigBrain' [1]. The visualization of the EC with its pre-α islands in the 'BigBrain' data set was performed using the supercomputer JURECA at Jülich Supercomputing Centre (JSC) [15]. Combined they enabled the visualization and in-depth analysis of the pre-α islands, their sizes, shapes, and underlying gray values in the reconstructed environment of the complete EC and the entire human brain.

2   Material and Methods

2.1   Histological Processing and 3D-Reconstruction of 'BigBrain'

In accordance with ethical requirements, a post-mortem human brain of a 65-year old male body donor with no medical history of neurological or mental illness was acquired during an autopsy performed under the body donor program of the University of Düsseldorf [1] (#4863). The brain was sectioned in the coronal plane (slice thickness: 20 μm) and stained for cell bodies using modified silver staining. 7404 sections were acquired and digitized with an in-plane resolution of 10 μm, then down-sampled to 20 μm and 3D-reconstructed, resulting in an isotropic resolution of 20 μm and a data set of about 1 TByte [1]. In addition, histological sections were digitized with high throughput bright-field microscopes (TissueScope LE120, Huron Digital Pathology), resulting in an in-plane resolution of 1 μm, which was used to verify the results at high-resolution. The image size for the latter was about 8–10 GByte per brain section image (8bit, bigtif format, uncompressed).

2.2   Border Definition and Annotation of the EC in A3D

The analysis of EC and adjacent regions was performed in high-resolution (1 μm) sections of the 'BigBrain' available in MicroDraw (The Institut Pasteur, Paris, France, https://github.com/r03ert0/microdraw) (Fig. 2). The cytoarchitectonic criteria for identifying the borders were based on previous cytoarchitectonic mappings of EC in ten post-mortem brains [16] according to criteria in literature [2, 17–21]. The EC was annotated in the images of the 3D-reconstructed 'BigBrain' (20 μm isotropic resolution)

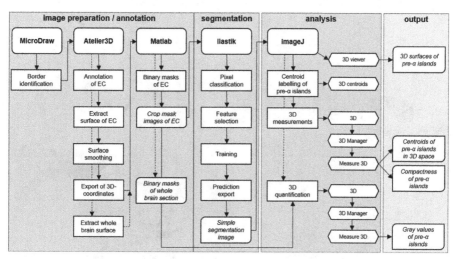

Fig. 2. Sequence and input/output data of the used programs. The rounded boxes indicate software tools, while square boxes indicate the main processing steps. Hexagons indicate plug-ins used in ImageJ (U.S. National Institutes of Health, USA) [24], while the half-square/angular boxes show the results of each process. The respective programs were used online in a browser, on a Windows operating system, on a Unix operating system, and in an HPC environment. Border identification in Microdraw (The Institut Pasteur, Paris, France, https://github.com/r03ert0/mic rodraw) was performed in sections of the 'BigBrain' with an in-plane resolution of 1 μm, while all other steps were performed in 3D based on the 3D-reconstructed 'BigBrain' sections with an isotropic resolution of 20 μm.

[1] using A3D [14] (Fig. 3). A3D was adapted in the framework of the international collaboration project 'BigBrain' to visualize and annotate the spatial data of the 3D reconstructed histological 'BigBrain' data set (https://bigbrainproject.org/hiball.html). As a result, 77 annotations in the left hemisphere (ID3, blue/dark) and 92 annotations in the right hemisphere (ID2, green/light) were obtained (Figs. 2 and 3). In general, every 25th section was annotated, but in cases where the 3D geometry, e.g. the thickness and total surface area of EC, changed considerably between the gaps of 25 sections, additional annotations were performed in every fifth section. A3D was then used to create gapless 3D structures from the original 2D annotations.

This resulted in individual 3D surface meshes of the EC of each hemisphere, computed in A3D (Fig. 2). The surfaces were checked for artifacts, iteratively adjusted, and corrected. The rough edges on the painted surfaces are delicately smoothed locally using normalized curvature operators in the normal direction [22, 23]. The smoothing method is applied on the 3D surfaces preserving their specific structures. This smoothing retains the area of the 3D triangular mesh as well as the volume inside the surface. It also avoids moving too far from the drawn points based on thresholds. Subsequently, the 3D Cartesian coordinates of EC surface contours were exported to be processed in MATLAB® (MathWorks, USA), with x-coordinates indicating the mediolateral (sagittal) axis, y-coordinates the dorsoventral (horizontal) axis, and the z-coordinates the rostrocaudal (coronal) axis (Fig. 3).

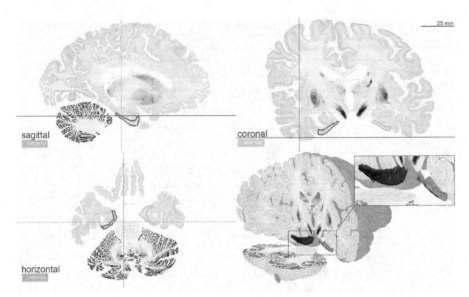

Fig. 3. Overview of the reconstructed sagittal, original coronal, and reconstructed horizontal section planes, as well as of the '3D view – volume' (bottom right) of the 'BigBrain' in A3D. EC of the left hemisphere dark, right hemisphere light. The EC is visualized as corresponding surfaces within the 3D 'BigBrain' model, with the surfaces magnified in the cutout for better visualization.

The coordinates of the surfaces resulted in dense binary masks of the EC and its pre-α islands. Furthermore, the coordinates were used to crop smaller parts of the whole brain images including EC (Fig. 2). In total, 1065 images for the left and 1063 images for the right hemisphere were cropped, resulting in a data set of about 1.2 GByte. Finally, a 3D median filter (r = 2px) was used to reduce the signal-to-noise ratio and emphasize the pre-α island boundaries.

2.3 Segmentation of Pre-α Islands in Ilastik

Segmentation of pre-α islands of the left and the right hemisphere was performed separately using the machine-learning based 'Pixel Classification' workflow of ilastik (European Molecular Biology Laboratory, Heidelberg, Germany) [25] (Fig. 2). After loading the cropped EC image stacks from A3D (20 μm isotropic resolution) and selecting all available descriptive image filters as features, a 'training' based on the Random Forest classifier was performed using training labeling for the classes background (Fig. 4, light) and pre-α islands (Fig. 4, dark). In total, training was performed per hemisphere on sixteen coronal (every 50th to 100th section), eight sagittal (every 100th section), and six horizontal (every 50th section) cropped EC sections. The 37 features include descriptors of pixel intensity (Gaussian Smoothing), edge-ness (Laplacian of Gaussian, Gaussian Gradient Magnitude, and Difference of Gaussians), and texture (Structure Tensor Eigenvalues, Hessian of Gaussian Eigenvalues) including their respective scales (σ: 0.3 (only Gaussian Smoothing), 0.7, 1, 1.6, 3.5, 5, and 10). The Random Forest classifier uses an ensemble of numerous individual decision trees, and here 100 trees were used, with a class prediction made for each tree individually (the class with the most votes being the prediction of the model) [25]. After completion of the training, segmented image stacks for the left hemisphere (1065 images, 8 bit, 898 × 712 pixels, 641 MByte) and right hemisphere (1063 images, 8 bit, 898 × 640 pixels, 583 MByte) of EC were exported (Fig. 4).

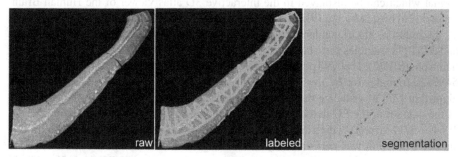

Fig. 4. Segmentation of pre-α islands in ilastik (here section number 700, left hemisphere). Training was performed with cropped EC images (left image), which were labeled (middle image) for the classes background (light) and pre-α islands (dark). The completion of the training resulted in segmented images (right image) showing the pre-α islands (dark) and background (light).

2.4 Analysis of Pre-α Islands in ImageJ

ImageJ was used to automatically quantify and describe the properties of the pre-α islands segmented with ilastik (Fig. 2). The detected pre-α islands were individually labeled and determined by their centroid coordinates. The analysis of the segmented pre-α islands in their 3D environment allowed to extract a set of parameters (e.g. 3D coordinates, volume, and compactness).

The compactness (range between 0 and 1) describes the ratio of pre-α islands volume and the smallest possible surrounding sphere including the individual pre-α islands. A value of 1 corresponds to a sphere and lower values to more complex structures.

Additionally, mean, mode, and standard deviation of the gray values were taken from the original 'BigBrain' images (8 bit, 20 μm resolution, unprocessed) at the corresponding positions of the segmented island. Cell islands that were smaller than five voxels (voxel size 20 μm isotropic) were removed based on the definition of islands as structures of three or more clustered neurons.

Finally, the mean gray values were inverted ($\bar{x}$(gray value) = 256-value), which resulted in lower and higher mean values corresponding to lower and higher cell-packing densities, respectively. Gradients of these gray values were plotted along the three main axes of the brain. Pearson correlations were computed including squared correlation coefficients, and the correlations were analyzed for significance. To exclude a possible bias of the gray level gradients due to the histological staining or the global correction of the intensities of the 'BigBrain' data set, the gray levels of the entire entorhinal cortex without the pre-α-islands were additionally determined. The pre-α islands of the cropped EC images were 3D visualized using the ImageJ '3D viewer' plug-in.

2.5 Visualization of the EC and the Included Pre-α Islands in the Context of the Entire 'BigBrain' Data Set

To visualize the EC and the included pre-α islands in the context of the entire 'BigBrain' data set, 2D segmentation images of both structures were stacked along the rostrocaudal axis to create 3D volumes (Fig. 2). These were subsequently converted to a custom data format which can be displayed in the interactive 3D atlas viewer of the Human Brain Project [26] hosted by the EBRAINS infrastructure (https://ebrains.eu/).

In addition, 3D triangular surface meshes (left hemisphere (ID3): 1886051 points and 3781098 triangles for islands, 2854912 points and 5709820 triangles for EC; right hemisphere (ID2): 1680293 points and 3369782 triangles for islands, 2743662 points and 5487320 triangles for EC) were extracted from the volumes using the marching cubes algorithm [27] to visualize the 3D appearance of the structures. Due to the large size of the data set of the EC in the whole BigBrain context (~37 GByte stack size, 6572 × 1064 × 5711 voxels), which did not allow for post-processing on classical desktop PCs, surface extraction was performed by subdividing the volumes into 3D chunks, which were then processed in parallel using the supercomputer system JURECA [15] at Jülich Supercomputing Centre (JSC).

3 Results

3.1 Overview of the Layers of the EC

The EC consists of six layers and almost cell free Substrata dissecantia (3 diss (external layer), 4 diss (internal layer) Figs. 1B, 5 and 6). Layer 2 harbored large stellate cells (modified pyramidal cells), forming pre-α islands of different size and shape, separated by neuropil.

In layer 3, pyramidal cells clustered into columns in the intermediate part of EC (Fig. 1B). The Substrata dissecantia continued in parallel to the pial surface: The rostral part of EC revealed only the external Substratum dissecans (3 diss) (Figs. 5 and 6), whereas the intermediate and caudal portions of EC showed both 3 diss and 4 diss (Fig. 1B–C). Layer 4 showed large and darkly stained neurons and was clearly visible along the rostrocaudal extent of EC. No clear border was visible between layer 5 and layer 6 as they often seemed to intermingle (Fig. 1B–C). The border between layer 6 and the white matter was distinct only in the intermediate to caudal parts of EC (Fig. 1B–C), but not rostrally.

Layer 2, Substrata dissecantia, and layer 4 of EC were specific to EC, but not to the neighboring structures. EC has borders with the amygdalopiriform transition area (APir), hippocampal-amygdaloid transition area (HATA), the parasubiculum (PaS), and BA35a (Figs. 5 and 6).

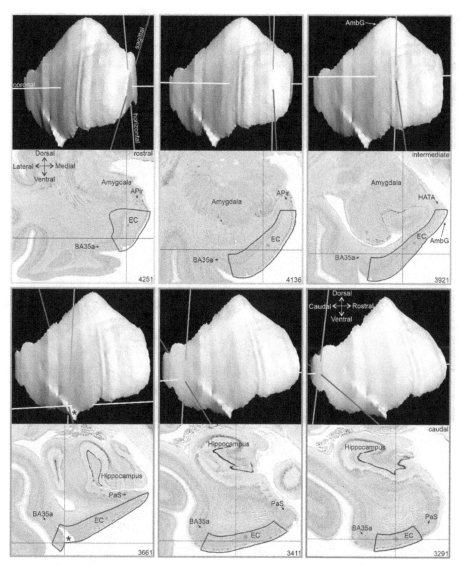

Fig. 5. 3D surface model of EC of the left hemisphere as computed in A3D (upper part of each frame) and corresponding annotation in coronal cytoarchitectonic section (lower image in each frame) from the rostral (top left) to the caudal (bottom right) extent of EC. The crosshairs in the cytoarchitectonic section show the exact position of the annotated EC within the 3D-reconstructed EC. The sagittal, horizontal, and coronal lines of the crosshairs correspond to the mediolateral, dorsoventral, and rostrocaudal plane, and the Cartesian x, y, and z coordinates, respectively. The EC has different neighboring areas along the rostrocaudal extent. Section numbers in the bottom right corner. Abbreviation: *AmbG*, ambient gyrus; *APir*, amygdalopiriform transition area; *BA35a*, Brodmann area 35a; *EC*, entorhinal cortex; *HATA*, hippocampal-amygdaloid transition area; *PaS*, parasubiculum [16]. *, incised and downward protruding cortex

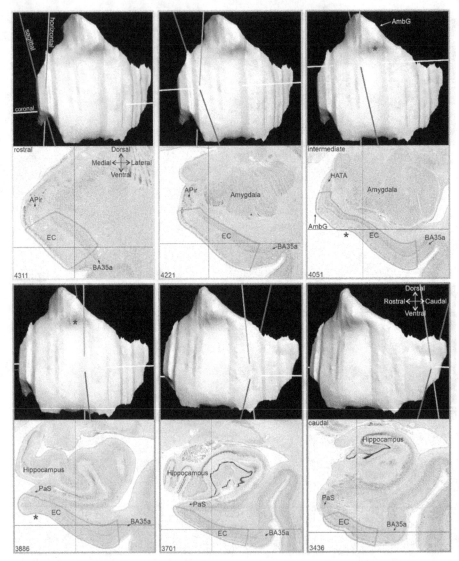

Fig. 6. 3D surface model of EC of the right hemisphere (designation as above for Fig. 5). *, intrarhinal sulcus [28]

3.2 Cytoarchitecture of Layer 2 (Pre-α Islands) and Modifications Along the Rostrocaudal Extent

The rostral part of EC showed the smallest (often narrow) pre-α islands separated from each other by little gaps (Fig. 1A). Neurons within the islands were more densely packed than in the rest of the EC. In the intermediate part of EC, pre-α islands were characterized by the largest size and the largest gap from the neighboring islands (Fig. 1B). In the caudal part of EC, pre-α islands were the most variable in their density and size (Fig. 1C). The three parts of EC differed from each other by the type of the predominantly found islands: small and round islands were found in the rostral part (which also showed a few narrow, elongated islands, Fig. 1A), elongated in the intermediate part, and round in the caudal part.

3.3 Surface and Morphological Features of Pre-α Islands in EC

Annotations for each hemisphere were stacked, smoothed while keeping the volume constant and visualized as 3D surfaces in A3D (Figs. 2, 5 and 6). On both sites, the EC shows the broadest extent in its intermediate part, while it becomes more compact in the most rostral and most caudal parts (Figs. 5 and 6). The peek in the intermediate part of EC belongs to the AmbG that is ventrally limited from the PhcG of EC by the intrarhinal sulcus [28]. The intrarhinal sulcus is clearly visible in the right hemisphere, where it can also be identified in the coronal sections (see asterisk in Fig. 6), while in the left hemisphere it was shallow (Fig. 5). The cortex of the left hemisphere was slightly damaged during the sectioning process of the paraffine embedded brain (see asterisk in Fig. 5). Therefore, an elevation of the surface could be observed in the 3D model (Fig. 5). This did not, however, affect the quality of the annotations and surface extractions of EC, as well as subsequent segmentation and analysis of pre-α islands (Fig. 7).

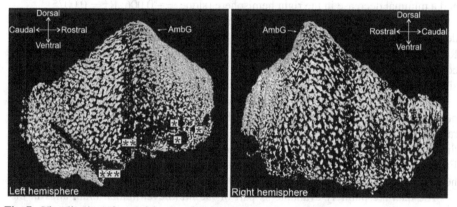

Fig. 7. Visualization of pre-α island surfaces in the EC: left and right hemispheres. The asterisks in the left hemisphere indicate regions with cutting artifacts: *, small cuts in the cortex; **, artifact of the digitally repaired 3D reconstruction of 'BigBrain'; ***, incised and downward protruding cortex. Abbreviation: *AmbG*, ambient gyrus

The 3D models of pre-α islands revealed a variety of different shapes. Three main groups were identified according to their measured compactness: round, elongated, and complex islands (Figs. 7 and 9). The comparison of the various shapes of the complex islands in 3D and the shapes seen in 2D histological sections indicated that the complex islands were composed of interconnected round and elongated ones that compose layer 2 of EC.

The pre-α island surfaces showed further structural differentiation (based on distribution, size, and shape of the islands) between the rostral, intermediate, and caudal parts of EC (Fig. 7). The rostral part showed the smallest and most densely packed pre-α islands of predominantly elongated and round shape. The intermediate part of EC was less densely packed than in its rostral part and revealed the largest islands with the widest gaps between them. In addition to elongated and round islands, the intermediate part showed the largest number of complex islands. The caudal part of EC included round and complex islands, which were larger and less densely packed than in the rostral part of EC, but more densely packed and smaller than in its intermediate part.

3.4   Number and Distribution of Pre-α Islands

In total, 2045 pre-α islands in the left and 1841 pre-α islands in the right hemisphere were found. In the following, a gradient of pre-α islands corresponds to the mean gray values for each pre-α islands as a correlate of their cell-packing density (Fig. 8).

The medial versus lateral gradient of pre-α islands indicated that the cell-packing density was higher in the lateral than in the medial EC, for both the left (slope $= 0.0058$; $R^2 = 0.0158$) and right hemispheres (slope $= -0.018$; $R^2 = 0.12$).

Regarding the dorsal to ventral gradient of pre-α islands, a slight increase in the cell-packing density was observed in the left hemisphere (slope $= 0.0198$; $R^2 = 0.0741$) and a minimal decrease in the right hemisphere (slope $= -0.006$; $R^2 = 0.0075$).

Finally, the gradient from caudal to rostral showed a slight decrease in cell-packing density in both the left (slope $= -0.0018$; $R^2 = 0.0015$) and right (slope $= -0.0049$; $R^2 = 0.0176$) hemispheres. All correlations were significant ($p < 0.05$), except the correlation along the dorsal-ventral axis of the left hemisphere, which did not reach significance ($p = 0.0840$).

The analysis of compactness showed that the morphology of pre-α islands varied between elongated, complex, and round, whereby the transitions between them were rather smooth (Fig. 9). Moreover, the histograms were left-skewed, indicating that there were more round and complex than elongated islands in EC of both hemispheres. Finally, the distribution of the different types of islands was highly comparable in both hemispheres.

The data are publicly available as part of the multilevel human brain atlas in the EBRAINS infrastructure and can be explored interactively in the EBRAINS 3D atlas viewer (https://atlases.ebrains.eu/viewer).

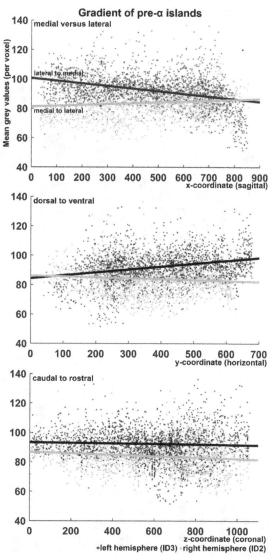

Fig. 8. Gradients of pre-α islands in EC, represented as mean gray values per pre-α islands, as a correlate of the cell-packing density within each island. Each ball (dark gray, left hemisphere; light gray, right hemisphere) represents a 3D centroid, thus a pre-α island. **Medial versus lateral** gradient: Note the difference between the hemispheres. Since the surfaces for each hemisphere were extracted separately and the values are sorted by their x-coordinates, the mean gray values in the left hemisphere are indicated from lateral to medial (outside to inside), while in the right hemisphere they are indicated from medial to lateral (inside to outside). **Dorsal to ventral** gradient: Note a longer line related to the left hemisphere, which is a reflection of an incised and downwards protruding cortex in the intermediate and caudal parts of the left EC (see asterisk in Figs. 5 and 7). **Caudal to rostral** gradient: Note that the z-coordinate goes from the most caudal (posterior) to the most rostral (anterior) coordinate.

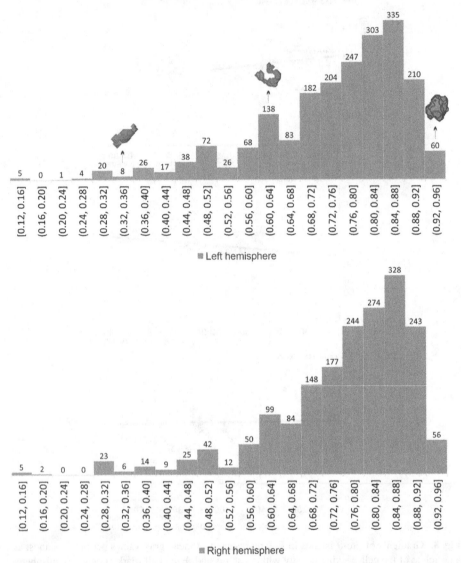

Fig. 9. Histogram indicating the frequency of compactness (from 0.12 to 1 in steps of 0.04) of pre-α islands in the left hemisphere (in total 2045 pre-α islands; upper histogram) and in the right hemisphere (in total 1841 pre-α islands; lower histogram) of the 'BigBrain' EC. For the left hemisphere, three examples are given for the different types of pre-α islands: one elongated (range of compactness (0.32, 0.36]), one complex (range of compactness (0.60, 0.64]) and one round (range of compactness (0.92, 0.96]) island.

4 Discussion

Based on the high-resolution data set of the 3D-reconstructed 'BigBrain' [1], we created a workflow that allowed a comprehensive analysis of the individual morphology and distribution of pre-α islands in layer 2 of the EC, by using existing and new software tools. The visualization and annotation software A3D was used to annotate the EC in both hemispheres, followed by the preparation of cropped EC images in MATLAB®. The machine-learning based 'Pixel Classification' tool of ilastik [25] was trained to identify and segment pre-α islands. ImageJ [24] was used to visualize the 3D surface of the segmented pre-α islands and to analyze individual pre-α islands in their spatial extent, including intensity and geometric measurements. Finally, whole brain section masks of the EC and the included pre-α islands were used to visualize the results in its native 3D environment employing marching cubes algorithm at the supercomputer system JURECA [15] at Jülich Supercomputing Centre (JSC). The required programs and the input and output files generated in each case are shown as a flowchart in Fig. 2.

The applications shown here using the 'BigBrain' data set enable a better understanding of the morphology of pre-α islands and a description of their underlying cytoarchitecture. Although pre-α islands exist only in the EC, there are other brain areas that show structures of distinct morphology. For example, the cell clusters of the amygdalopiriform transition area, for which our workflow, i.e. the annotation in A3D, labeling of structures in ilastik, and their 3D visualization in ImageJ, could be applied or adapted.

By focusing on the morphological characteristics of pre-α islands in the 'BigBrain' model, numerous islands of a specific shape were analyzed. Compactness analysis, performed for the first time at high-resolution in 3D space, revealed round and complex islands as the predominant island types. In addition, 3D characterization of pre-α islands using the 'BigBrain' model allowed the identification of differences based on the distribution, size, and shape of islands in the rostral, intermediate, and caudal part of EC. Here, the largest number of complex islands was observed in the intermediate part of EC. Previous approaches indicated the complexity of the pre-α islands by reporting "bridges" [8, 12, 13]. However, the analysis of complex islands based on 2D images is complicated and error-prone because they do not allow following islands between sectional planes. Thus, classical histological 2D analysis can only provide a limited description of the 3D shape and size of pre-α islands. As a result, the number of complex islands observed in 2D sections is lower than the number obtained from 3D analyses.

Regarding interhemispheric differences in the layer 2 characteristics, the present study found more pre-α islands in the left than in the right hemisphere by comparing the numbers of 3D centroids (i.e. pre-α islands) that were exported from ImageJ. Although this result is based on only one human brain, it is supported by a previous study that found a higher number of pre-α neurons in the left than in the right EC, in 18 out of 22 human brains analyzed [21].

To our knowledge, density gradients based on intensity measurements, in particular, gray values corresponding to the cell packing densities, of all pre-α islands embedded in layer 2 of EC have not been discussed or raised in previous studies. Nevertheless, previous cytoarchitectonic and immunohistochemical studies are in support of the present results on the rostral to caudal increase of cell packing density. Heinsen et al., 1994 [21], observed such a gradient on the basis of sections Nissl-stained with gallocyanin, whereas Beall and Lewis (1992) [29] described increases towards the caudal extent of EC based on light transmittance of phosphorylated neurofilament protein immunoreactivities. Interestingly, anatomical and electrophysiological studies regarding the hippocampus provided evidence for a gradient along its dorsoventral axis in rodents, while gene expression studies indicated distinct functional domains with often clearly demarcated borders [30]. These observations led to the conclusion that the well-known view that spatial navigation and memory, and thus cognitive functions, are mediated in the dorsal (or posterior) parts of the hippocampus, whereas emotional responses are mediated in its ventral (or anterior) part, should be reconsidered. It is now proposed that hippocampal functional gradients may be superimposed on distinct functional domains at both the anatomical and mRNA levels [30]. Regarding the functional topography of the EC, Navarro Schröder et al., 2015 [31], performed a high-field functional MRI study (at 7 T) in which two groups of independent participants were presented with either images of scenes (for spatial stimuli) or images of objects (for non-spatial stimuli). They showed evidence of functional division along the anteroposterior axis, as the anterior EC showed higher responses to non-spatial stimuli and the posterior EC showed higher responses to spatial stimuli. It would be interesting to investigate whether there is a functional gradient along the rostrocaudal (anteroposterior) axis of EC that correlates with the density gradients we found in the present study. Finally, whether these then correlate with the proposed gradients along the hippocampal long axis.

Previous cytoarchitectonic studies subdivided the EC based on the differences found in all layers (into two subareas in Brodmann (1909) [7] to eight subareas in Insausti et al., 1995, 2017 [2, 17]). However, the present study describes the heterogeneity of pre-α islands at the level confined to one layer, layer 2. In the intermediate and caudal parts of EC, we identified conspicuous islands of different shapes (our complex islands) in addition to the island types described by Insausti et al., 1995 [2]. These islands were not clearly separated from each other and appeared to be composed of interconnected islands of other types, resulting in a complex morphology. Braak and Braak (1992) [8] identified three major subareas (medial, lateral, and central), based on specific features of entorhinal layers in different parts of EC. The authors considered bipartition of pre-α and pre-β layer (layer 2 and 3 of Zilles (1987) [4]) as a criterion for the medial subarea which covered the ambient gyrus. Moreover, a characteristic tripartition of the pri-α layer (layer 4 of Zilles (1987) [4]) marked their central subarea, which covered a part of the parahippocampal gyrus [8]. In contrast, based on the distribution of pre-α islands, the present study suggests that the ambient gyrus partly comprises the rostral and intermediate parts of EC.

However, since only one 'BigBrain' was analyzed as a use case in the present study, but 3D-reconstructions of two other 'BigBrains' are currently under development, we intend to apply our workflow to these 'BigBrain' models. This will facilitate visualization of pre-α island surfaces and further descriptive analyses, but could also enable quantitative analysis of possible EC subareas. Further application of the method presented here to other high-resolution brain models will also allow continued investigation of the interindividual variability of pre-α islands at the highest resolution level.

Taken together, the present study demonstrated a new workflow for data analysis and visualization of EC and its embedded pre-α islands using machine-learning based and image data analysis tools. With these tools, we demonstrated new characteristics of the human EC and pre-α islands embedded therein, in particular the existence of complex islands and the rostral to caudal cell-packing density gradient. As pre-α cells of EC are involved in the functionally important perforant pathway, it becomes clear why it is so important to understand the natural structure of EC in order to detect possible changes during aging and in neuro-/psychiatric diseases. The results of this study will be made available to the neuroscientific community via the research infrastructure EBRAINS and will be linked to the multilevel human brain atlas of EBRAINS. The representation of the surfaces of the EC and the islands contained therein is of particular interest to a broad readership. The first-time visualization of these microscopic structures in the context of the entire brain represents an important bridge between basic research and possible medical applications, as it is common in medicine to view the brain in its natural three-dimensional environment. Our current results could provide a reference model for future studies of neurodegenerative and psychiatric diseases such as Alzheimer's, Parkinson's, and schizophrenia.

Acknowledgments. This project has received funding from the European Union's Horizon 2020 Framework Programme for Research and Innovation under the Specific Grant Agreement No. 945539 (Human Brain Project SGA3). This work was also funded by Helmholtz Association's Initiative and Networking Fund through the Helmholtz International BigBrain Analytics and Learning Laboratory (HIBALL) under the Helmholtz International Lab grant agreement InterLabs-0015. Computing time was granted through JARA on the supercomputer JURECA at Jülich Supercomputing Centre (JSC).

References

1. Amunts, K., et al.: BigBrain: an ultrahigh-resolution 3D human brain model. Science **340**(6139), 1472–1475 (2013)
2. Insausti, R., Tunon, T., Sobreviela, T., Insausti, A.M., Gonzalo, L.M.: The human entorhinal cortex: a cytoarchitectonic analysis. J. Comp. Neurol. **355**(2), 171–198 (1995)
3. Braak, H.: Zur Pigmentarchitektonik der Großhirnrinde des Menschen. Z. Zellforsch. Mikrosk. Anat. **127**(3), 407–438 (1972)
4. Zilles K.: Graue und weiße Substanz des Hirnmantels. Anatomie des Menschen In Georg Thieme Verlag, Stuttgart, pp. 382–471 (1987)
5. Rose, M.: Der Allocortex bei Tier und Mensch I. Teil J. Psychol. Neurol. **34**, 1–111 (1927)
6. Lorente de Nó, R.: Studies on the structure of the cerebral cortex. II. Continuation of the study of the ammonic system. J. für Psychologie und Neurologie (1934)
7. Brodmann, K.: Vergleichende Lokalisationslehre der Grosshirnrinde in ihren Prinzipien dargestellt auf Grund des Zellenbaues. Barth (1909)
8. Braak, H., Braak, E.: The human entorhinal cortex: normal morphology and lamina-specific pathology in various diseases. Neurosci. Res. **15**(1–2), 6–31 (1992)
9. Duvernoy, H.M.: The Human Hippocampus: Functional Anatomy, Vascularization and Serial Sections with MRI. Springer, Heidelberg (2005). https://doi.org/10.1007/b138576
10. Gómez-Isla, T., Price, J.L., McKeel, D.W., Jr., Morris, J.C., Growdon, J.H., Hyman, B.T.: Profound loss of layer II entorhinal cortex neurons occurs in very mild Alzheimer's disease. J. Neurosci. **16**(14), 4491–4500 (1996)

11. Braak, H., Braak, E.: Neuropathological stageing of Alzheimer-related changes. Acta Neuropathol. **82**(4), 239–259 (1991)
12. Braak, H.: Architectonics of the Human Telecephalic Cortex. Springer, Heidelberg (1980)
13. Hevner, R.F., Wong-Riley, M.T.: Entorhinal cortex of the human, monkey, and rat: metabolic map as revealed by cytochrome oxidase. J. Comp. Neurol. **326**(3), 451–469 (1992)
14. Borgeat, L., Godin, G., Massicotte, P., Poirier, G., Blais, F., Beraldin, J.A.: Visualizing and analyzing the Mona Lisa. IEEE Comput. Graph. Appl. **27**(6), 60–68 (2007)
15. Krause, D., Thörnig, P.: Jureca: Modular supercomputer at jülich supercomputing centre. J. Large-Scale Res. Facil. JLSRF **4**, 132 (2018)
16. Amunts, K., et al.: Cytoarchitectonic mapping of the human amygdala, hippocampal region and entorhinal cortex: intersubject variability and probability maps. Anat. Embryol. **210**(5), 343–352 (2005)
17. Insausti, R., Muñoz-López, M., Insausti, A.M., Artacho-Pérula, E.: The human periallocortex: layer pattern in presubiculum, parasubiculum and entorhinal cortex. A review. Front. Neuroanat. **11**, 84 (2017)
18. Ding, S.L., Van Hoesen, G.W.: Borders, extent, and topography of human perirhinal cortex as revealed using multiple modern neuroanatomical and pathological markers. Hum. Brain Mapp. **31**(9), 1359–1379 (2010)
19. Braak, H., Braak, E.: On areas of transition between entorhinal allocortex and temporal isocortex in the human brain. Normal morphology and lamina-specific pathology in Alzheimer's disease. Acta Neuropathol. **68**(4), 325–332 (1985)
20. Krimer, L.S., Hyde, T.M., Herman, M.M., Saunders, R.C.: The entorhinal cortex: an examination of cyto-and myeloarchitectonic organization in humans. Cereb. Cortex **7**(8), 722–731 (1997)
21. Heinsen, H., et al.: Quantitative investigations on the human entorhinal area: left-right asymmetry and age-related changes. Anat. Embryol. **190**(2), 181–194 (1994)
22. Desbrun, M., Meyer, M., Schröder, P., Barr, A.H.: Implicit fairing of irregular meshes using diffusion and curvature flow. In: Proceedings of the 26th Annual Conference on Computer Graphics and Interactive Techniques, pp. 317–324 (1999)
23. Kroon, D.J.: Smooth triangulated mesh. MATLAB Central File Exchange (2019). https://www.mathworks.com/matlabcentral/fileexchange/26710-smooth-triangulated-mesh
24. Schneider, C.A., Rasband, W.S., Eliceiri, K.W.: NIH Image to ImageJ: 25 years of image analysis. Nat. Methods **9**(7), 671–675 (2012)
25. Berg, S., et al.: ilastik: interactive machine learning for (bio)image analysis. Nat. Methods **16**(12), 1226–1232 (2019)
26. Amunts K., et al.: The human brain project—synergy between neuroscience, computing, informatics, and brain-inspired technologies. PLoS Biol **17**(7), e3000344 (2019)
27. Lewiner, T., Lopes, H., Vieira, A.W., Tavares, G.: Efficient implementation of marching cubes' cases with topological guarantees. J. Graph. Tools **8**(2), 1–15 (2003)
28. Insausti, R., Córcoles-Parada, M., Ubero, M.M., Rodado, A., Insausti, A.M., Muñoz-López, M.: Cytoarchitectonic areas of the gyrus ambiens in the human brain. Front. Neuroanat. **13**, 21 (2019)
29. Beall, M.J., Lewis, D.A.: Heterogeneity of layer II neurons in human entorhinal cortex. J. Comp. Neurol. **321**(2), 241–266 (1992)

30. Strange, B.A., Witter, M.P., Lein, E.S., Moser, E.I.: Functional organization of the hippocampal longitudinal axis. Nat. Rev. Neurosci. **15**(10), 655–669 (2014)
31. Schröder, T.N., Haak, K.V., Jimenez, N.I.Z., Beckmann, C.F., Doeller, C.F.: Functional topography of the human entorhinal cortex. Elife **4**, e06738 (2015)

Deep Learning-Supported Cytoarchitectonic Mapping of the Human Lateral Geniculate Body in the BigBrain

Andrea Brandstetter[1](✉), Najoua Bolakhrif[1], Christian Schiffer[1,2](✉), Timo Dickscheid[1,2], Hartmut Mohlberg[1], and Katrin Amunts[1,3]

[1] Institute of Neuroscience and Medicine (INM-1), Research Centre Jülich, Jülich, Germany
{a.brandstetter,c.schiffer}@fz-juelich.de
[2] Helmholtz AI, Research Centre Jülich, Jülich, Germany
[3] C. and O. Vogt Institute for Brain Research, University Hospital Düsseldorf, Medical Faculty, Heinrich Heine University Düsseldorf, Düsseldorf, Germany

Abstract. The human lateral geniculate body (LGB) with its six sickle shaped layers (lam) represents the principal thalamic relay nucleus for the visual system. Cytoarchitectonic analysis serves as the groundtruth for multimodal approaches and studies exploring its function. This technique, however, requires experienced knowledge about human neuroanatomy and is costly in terms of time. Here we mapped the six layers of the LGB manually in serial, histological sections of the BigBrain, a high-resolution model of the human brain, whereby their extent was manually labeled in every 30th section in both hemispheres. These maps were then used to train a deep learning algorithm in order to predict the borders on sections in-between these sections. These delineations needed to be performed in 1 μm scans of the tissue sections, for which no exact cross-section alignment is available. Due to the size and number of analyzed sections, this requires to employ high-performance computing. Based on the serial section delineations, high-resolution 3D reconstruction was performed at 20 μm isotropic resolution of the BigBrain model. The 3D reconstruction shows the shape of the human LGB and its sublayers for the first time at cellular precision. It represents a use case to study other complex structures, to visualize their shape and relationship to neighboring structures. Finally, our results could provide reference data of the LGB for modeling and simulation to investigate the dynamics of signal transduction in the visual system.

Keywords: Lateral geniculate body (LGB) · Corpus geniculatum laterale (CGL) · BigBrain · Deep learning · 3D reconstruction · Cytoarchitecture

1 Introduction

The lateral geniculate body (LGB, *lat.* Corpus geniculatum laterale, from now on LGB) plays a key role in visual perception. Together with the medial geniculate body, which is involved in auditive processing, both nuclei constitute the metathalamus. The LGB is

K. Amunts et al. (Eds.): BrainComp 2019, LNCS 12339, pp. 22–32, 2021.
https://doi.org/10.1007/978-3-030-82427-3_2

located on the ventral surface of the brain. It mainly receives connections from the retina via the optic tract, but also from layer 6 of the visual cortex and the reticular nucleus of the thalamus [1]. The most prominent efferent projections reach the primary visual cortex, i.e. Brodmann's area 17 (or area V1, or hOc1 [2]; via the optic radiation (Fig. 1 top image) [1]. The human LGB consists of six layers. The two most ventrally located layers (layers 1 and 2) consist of larger neurons and are known as magnocellular, while layers 3 to 6 are parvocellular layers (Fig. 1 bottom image). Koniocellular neurons are located in between those laminae.

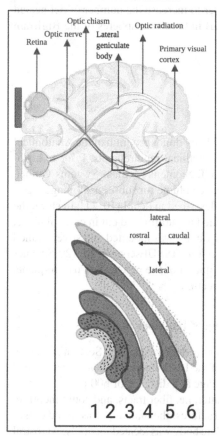

Fig. 1. The human visual pathway (top image). The location of the lateral geniculate body (LGB) is marked by the black rectangle. Six layers of the LGB (bottom image) describing contralateral projections depicted in green and ipsilateral projections in red. Created with BioRender.com (Color figure online)

Layers 2, 3 and 5 receive fibers from the ipsilateral eye, whereas layers 1, 4 and 6 receive fibers from the contralateral eye [3]. I.e., each layer receives information from one eye only. Later on, the information will be merged to be processed and interpreted as a binocular image in the visual cortex [4]. Approximately 80% of the retinal information derive from midget ganglion cells and are transferred to the parvocellular neurons in the LGB in layers 3 to 6. These small neurons are specialized in object and detail recognition due to their ability of generating a high spatial resolution and red-green color vision [4]. Midget cells are characterized as small, color-sensitive slow adapting cells from the retina, contrary to parasol cells. Retinal parasol cells send impulses to the bigger magnocellular layers 1 and 2, which are functional for time resolution and hence for the perception of position and movement [5]. Non-Midget-non-Parasol ganglion cells from the retina project to koniocellular neurons of the LGB, which further project to the primary visual cortex, similarly to the parvo- and magnocellular systems. Since the LGB transfers retinal information directly to the primary visual cortex via the optic radiation, it is also defined as first-order relay [1]. The koniocellular neurons most probably play a role in color perception [4]. The middle part of the LGB in coronal sections is called the hilum, and the taperings at the medial and lateral ends of the LGB are called the medial and lateral horn of the LGB, respectively [6].

Lesions in the LGB can affect the function of the visual pathway. For example, patients suffering from multiple sclerosis or Alzheimer's disease show a general volume loss of the LGB, indicating in the latter case a significant relation between degeneration of the LGB and amyloid-β pathology [7, 8]. After loss of visual experience due to an injury of the primary visual cortex but with an intact LGB, certain visual information processing still exists. This phenomenon discovered by functional magnetic resonance imaging (fMRI) is called blindsight [9].

This work aims to map the LGB and its layers at microscopical resolution, to provide reference data for studies targeting the LGB in the living human brain, to develop a use case enabling the combination of expert annotations based on cytoarchitectonic criteria in a subset of sections with deep learning in order to increase the number of delineated sections. A 3D reconstruction of the human LGB in both hemispheres of the BigBrain dataset was computed and visualized [10].

2 Materials and Methods

2.1 Histology

The BigBrain (65-year-old male) comes from the body donor program of the Anatomical Institute of Düsseldorf in accordance to legal and ethical requirements. Prior to histological processing MRI images were taken (1.5 T, Siemens Medical Systems GmbH, Erlangen, Germany) in order to provide a reference volume for subsequent image registration. Histological processing was previously described in detail [10, 11]. In short, the brain was fixed in 4% buffered formalin, embedded in paraffin and cut in coronal plane, each Sect. 20 μm thick. Every section – of total 7404 – was mounted and silver stained for cell bodies. The sections were digitized using a TISSUEscope™ LE120 Scanner (Huron Digital Pathology) [10]. The spatial resolution of the images is 1 μm in-plane, the average size of the images is 10 GByte per section.

2.2 Manual Analysis and Reference Mapping of Histological Sections

High-resolution images were analyzed and manually delineated using SectionTracer, an online tool written in JavaScript [12]. Borders of the LGB and its six layers were traced in 16 sections per hemisphere, i.e. every 30th image at a distance of 600 μm.

The human LGB is surrounded by white matter, i.e. fiber tracts, and could therefore be clearly distinguished from its neighboring structures: the thalamus was found dorsomedially from the LGB while the medial geniculate body was located medially. At rostral levels the LGB was completely surrounded by white matter.

The borders of the six layers of the LGB were identified based on differences in the cytoarchitecture (Fig. 2). Magno- and parvocellular layers were mainly distinguished according to their cell-size and -density. The pale koniocellular neurons served as main indicators for the borders between the different layers of the LGB. Wherever these criteria were not sufficient, i.e. where two parvocellular layers were not separated by a koniocellular lamina, cytoarchitectonic criteria such as size, shape, density and distribution of neurons were applied. Borders were drawn where the cytoarchitectonic pattern changed. Layers were numbered according to their position, starting from the most ventral layer 1 at the brain surface, increasing to the uppermost dorsal layer 6.

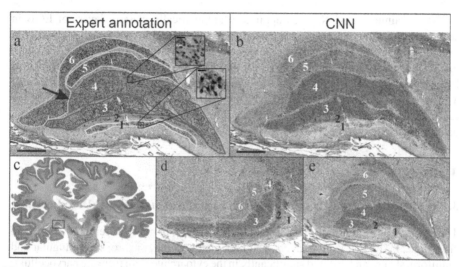

Fig. 2. Shape and borders of the six layers (labeled by different colors and numbers) of the human lateral geniculate body (LGB) on coronal sections. Upper row shows a comparison between manual expert mapping (a) and the prediction of the CNN (b). The location of the LGB on the coronal section is shown in (c). One caudal (d) and one rostral section (e) indicate different shapes of the LGB at different levels of sectioning. Scale bars: a–b, c–e 1 mm, c 20 mm. Scalebar magnification in a: 50 μm.

The volumes of the LGB and its layers were measured using Cavalieri's principle. A shrinkage factor of 1,931 was used for calculations in order to consider the shrinkage occurring during histological processing, the fixation, respectively [13].

The layers were then 3D reconstructed and transferred to the BigBrain space, which has a spatial resolution of 20 μm isotropic [12]. Results were visualized using the software ParaView [14, 15].

2.3 Training of the Deep-Learning Algorithm to Predict Missing Delineations

A convolutional neural network (CNN) was trained to classify each image pixel according to each lamina of the LGB. Network architecture and training procedure were based on Schiffer et al. [16], as they have been used successfully to aid mapping of cytoarchitectonic areas in several cortical brain regions [17–20].

The workflow uses a U-shape architecture for brain area segmentation with two encoder branches capturing the input data at different spatial scales. Training and prediction was controlled by the web-based interface of the tool, and performed remotely on the supercomputer JURECA [21] at Jülich Supercomputing Centre (JSC). The training time on the HPC system was around 70 min.

After training, the CNN was applied to automatically classify layers of LGB in sections without annotations. Automatically created annotations were quality-checked to exclude misclassified sections. Annotations were then non-linearly transformed [22] into the 3D reconstructed BigBrain space [10]. Previously excluded sections were replaced by interpolation [23]. Finally, the marching cubes algorithm [24] was applied to extract a surface mesh for each layer of LGB. This 3D reconstruction step is not part of the tool provided by [16], but it follows directly the experimental protocol for the BigBrain dataset described therein.

3 Results

3.1 Cytoarchitectonic Mapping Based on Expert Annotations and Deep Learning

The analysis of the LGB allowed to identify six layers, partially different in shape and size (Fig. 2). The two ventral layers contained magnocellular neurons of triangular and multiform shapes and differed significantly in the cytoarchitecture from the parvocellular layers 3–6. Layers 1 and 2 were thinner and more elongated; contained round and oval shaped neurons. Layers 3 and 6 were most prominent and were reached over a larger distance than the other two layers of the parvocellular part. Layer 5 was the shortest and least developed layer with respect to its mediolateral extent. On most sections, the layers were separated by a white koniocellular line, characterized by a low cell density. On a few sections, layers 1 and 4 as well as 4 and 6 were connected. The same was true for layers 2 and 3 as well as 3 and 5, where the koniocellular lines were lacking (Fig. 2a, black arrow). Although layers 1 and 2 were the thinnest structures, the magnocellular neurons are clearly visible, due to the magnocellular neurons (Fig. 2a, inset). Layers 3 to 6, on the other hand, were composed of smaller and more densely packed cells. The neurons on the lateral and medial horn of the LGB in each layer were loosely packed, while the neurons at the hilum were denser.

In total, 13 sections were labeled by an expert in the left hemisphere and 11 sections in the right hemisphere, with a distance of 0.6 mm. The LGB of the left hemisphere was found and processed by the CNN on 366 sections (rostro-caudal extent 7.3 mm) and on 293 coronal sections (extent of 5.9 mm) of the right hemisphere. For comparison between the expert annotation and the prediction of the CNN see Fig. 2a and b.

3.2 High-Resolution 3D Reconstruction

The exact location of the human LGB is depicted in the BigBrain model in Fig. 3a. A high-resolution 3D reconstruction was performed to get a deeper insight into the complex shape of the human LGB. The prominent hilum and the elongated lateral horn are characteristic for the shape of the human LGB (Fig. 3b). In more detail, the dorsal surface of the LGB is mainly covered by layers 4, 5 and 6. Layer 4 is more prominent at the hilum and the medial horn (Fig. 3b), while layer 3 is most prominent at the lateral horn (Fig. 3c). Most parts of the ventral surface of the LGB are covered by layer 1 medially and by layer 2 laterally (Fig. 3c).

3.3 Volumes of Layers

The total volumes of the LGB, after consideration of the shrinkage factor, are 120.5 mm^3 on the left, and 113.2 mm^3 on the right hemisphere (Table 1). The parvocellular layers are bigger than the magnocellular layers. The total volume of the LGB is 141.2 on the left, and 132.2 mm^3 on the right hemisphere. It contains the six layers, but also koniocellular layers and blood vessels, which are not included in the volumes of the single layers.

Table 1. Volumes (in mm^3) of each of the layer of the lateral geniculate body (LGB) in both hemispheres, sum of layers 1–6, and total volume.

LGB	Left [mm^3]	Right [mm^3]
Layer 1	10.2	7.8
Layer 2	8.3	7.4
Layer 3	28.5	27.4
Layer 4	25.9	21.3
Layer 5	20.2	21.8
Layer 6	27.4	27.5
Σ of layers 1–6	120.5	113.2
Total	141.2	132.2

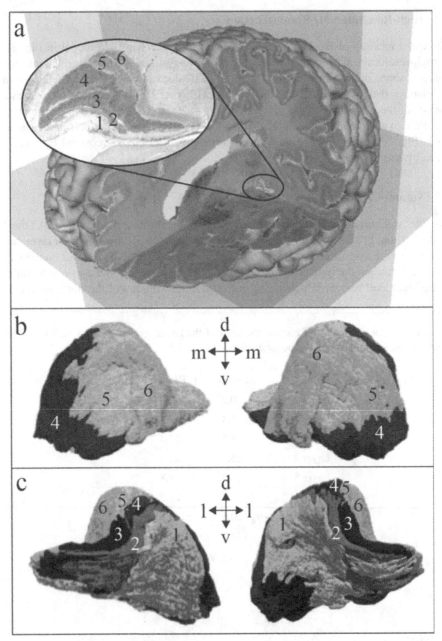

Fig. 3. 3D reconstruction of the lateral geniculate body (LGB). **(a)** Localization of the left lateral geniculate body (LGB) in the BigBrain model. **(b-c)** Surface of the reconstructed left and right LGB revealing its specific shape and its different layers. **(b)** dorso-caudal view **(c)** ventro-rostral view. Abbreviations: d = dorsal, l = lateral, m = medial, v = ventral.

4 Discussion and Conclusion

This study presents the first application for mapping a complex subcortical gray matter structure, the LGB, combining an expert-based and a deep-learning approach, resulting in a high-resolution 3D reconstruction of the LGB in the BigBrain template. It shows, for the first time, the shape of the individual six layers in 3D space while previous information was mainly obtained from 2D sections. The maps are publicly available in the EBRAINS multilevel human brain atlas (https://ebrains.eu/service/human-brain-atlas), where they can be explored in an interactive 3D viewer (https://interactive-viewer.apps.hbp.eu/saneUrl/BigBrain_LGB) and can be found under the DOI: https://doi.org/10.25493/33Z0-BX.

Due to the large size of the human brain, subcortical nuclei such as the LGB and cortical areas are found in tens to hundreds to thousands of sections, in dependence on the size of the structure. To map a structure manually in every section using traditional methods becomes impossible when structures are complex or large. As an alternative option, the extent of the structures can be interpolated. The drawback of this method is that images have to be 3D reconstructed before further processing [16]. Herein, we provide a use case using a semi-automated prediction of borders supported by deep learning. The algorithm learns from manually annotated borders and is able to use this knowledge for annotating the same area in previously unseen sections. Since it directly interprets the texture and brain topology, it is much more precise than a 3D interpolation in the reconstructed space and allows to use unregistered single sections.

Due to the large number of images and large size of the sections, training and application of the CNN was performed on the supercomputer system JURECA [18] at Jülich Supercomputing Centre (JSC). The use of high-performance computers becomes even more relevant when larger structures are being analyzed in whole brain sections. While computation in the LGB was completed in 2 h, comparable computations for the thalamus, for example, would take 50 h. Existing work on automatic classification of cytoarchitectonic cortical areas [16] also indicate that computational effort increases considerably when trying to automatically identify larger brain regions with more complex cytoarchitectonic and morphological properties.

Our findings of the total volume of the LGB, shrinkage factor included, is in line with previous findings. Andrews and colleagues reported mean LGB volumes of 121 mm^3 for the right and 115 mm^3 for the left hemisphere; the variance was quite high and ranged from 91.1 to 157 mm^3 for both hemispheres [25]. Further investigations in additional brains in the future would help to better understand intersubject variability in terms of the size and/or shape of the LGB.

High-resolution mapping data of the LGB may open a broad field of applications. For example, routine Magnetic Resonance Imaging (MRI) studies often lack sufficient contrast and/or spatial resolution and could benefit from such atlas data. Current studies on the implementation of electrically stimulated prostheses in the visual cortex aim to restore part of the vision in blind people by multiple stimulations of electrodes to percept light [26, 27], where such maps could be applied in the future to increase the localization accuracy. The investigation of the pathomechanisms of diseases where the visual pathway is affected, such as Multiple Sclerosis or glaucoma could be supported by the maps [28, 29]. The maps provide input data for modelling and simulation of different types of neurons, neuronal pathways or networks using platforms like *The Virtual Brain* [30]. With respect to basic neuroscience, the visualization and differentiation of the layers is expected to contribute to a more in-depth analysis of information processing in visual pathways. The present approach provides a use case for application in other brain areas and brains of other species enabling a fast and detailed prediction of the extent of small and complex structures, including visualization and volume analyses, with a minimum of manual effort and time expenditure.

Acknowledgements. This project has received funding from the European Union's Horizon 2020 Framework Programme for Research and Innovation under the Specific Grant Agreement No. 945539 (Human Brain Project SGA3). This work was also funded by Helmholtz Association's Initiative and Networking Fund through the Helmholtz International BigBrain Analytics and Learning Laboratory (HIBALL) under the Helmholtz International Lab grant agreement InterLabs-0015. Computing time was granted through JARA on the supercomputer JURECA at Jülich Supercomputing Centre (JSC).

References

1. Sherman, S.M., Guillery, R.W.: The role of the thalamus in the flow of information to the cortex. Philos Trans. R. Soc. B Biol. Sci. **357**(1428), 1695–1708 (2002). https://doi.org/10.1098/rstb.2002.1161

2. Amunts, K., Malikovic, A., Mohlberg, H., Schormann, T., Zilles, K.: Brodmann's areas 17 and 18 brought into stereotaxic space - where and how variable? Neuroimage **11**(1), 66–84 (2000). https://doi.org/10.1006/nimg.1999.0516

3. Duggan, W.F.: Anatomy of the eye and orbit. Arch. Ophthalmol. **10**(5), 723–724 (1933). https://doi.org/10.1001/archopht.1933.00830060147017

4. Eiber, C.D., et al.: Receptive field properties of koniocellular on/off neurons in the lateral geniculate nucleus of marmoset monkeys. J. Neurosci. **38**(48), 10384–10398 (2018). https://doi.org/10.1523/JNEUROSCI.1679-18.2018

5. Purves, D.: Neuroscience, 5th edn. Sinauer Associates Inc., Sunderland (2012)

6. Prasad, S., Galetta, S.L.: Anatomy and physiology of the afferent visual system. Handbook of Clinical Neurology, vol. 102 (2011)

7. Papadopoulou, A., et al.: Damage of the lateral geniculate nucleus in MS. Neurology **92**(19), e2240–e2249 (2019). https://doi.org/10.1212/WNL.0000000000007450

8. Erskine, D., et al.: Changes to the lateral geniculate nucleus in Alzheimer's disease but not dementia with Lewy bodies. Neuropathol. Appl. Neurobiol. **42**(4), 366–376 (2016). https://doi.org/10.1111/nan.12249

9. Schmid, M.C., et al.: Blindsight depends on the lateral geniculate nucleus. Nature **466**(7304), 373–377 (2010). https://doi.org/10.1038/nature09179

10. Amunts, K., et al.: BigBrain: an ultrahigh-resolution 3D human brain model. Science (80-) **340**(6139), 1472–1475 (2013). https://doi.org/10.1126/science.1235381

11. Amunts, K., Zilles, K.: Architectonic mapping of the human brain beyond Brodmann. Neuron **88**(6), 1086–1107 (2015). https://doi.org/10.1016/j.neuron.2015.12.001

12. Amunts, K., Mohlberg, H., Bludau, S., Zilles, K.: Julich-Brain: a 3D probabilistic atlas of the human brain's cytoarchitecture. Science (80-) **369**(6506), 988–992 (2020). https://doi.org/10.1126/science.abb4588

13. Amunts, K., Schleicher, A., Zilles, K.: Cytoarchitecture of the cerebral cortex-more than localization. Neuroimage **37**(4), 1061–1065 (2007). https://doi.org/10.1016/j.neuroimage.2007.02.037
14. Ahrens, J., Geveci, B., Law, C.: ParaView: an end-user tool for large data visualization. www.paraview.org. Accessed 11 Feb 2021
15. The ParaView Guide | ParaView. https://www.paraview.org/paraview-guide/. Accessed Feb 11 2021
16. Schiffer, C., et al.: Convolutional neural networks for cytoarchitectonic brain mapping at large scale, November 2020. http://arxiv.org/abs/2011.12857. Accessed 20 Dec 2020
17. EBRAINS - Ultrahigh resolution 3D cytoarchitectonic map of Area hOc1 (V1, 17, CalcS) created by a Deep-Learning assisted workflow. https://search.kg.ebrains.eu/instances/Dataset/696d6062-3b86-498f-9ca6-e4d67b433396. Accessed 6 Mar 2021
18. EBRAINS - Ultrahigh resolution 3D cytoarchitectonic map of Area hOc2 (V2, 18) created by a Deep-Learning assisted workflow. https://search.kg.ebrains.eu/instances/Dataset/63093617-9b72-45f5-88e6-f648ad05ae79. Accessed 6 Mar 2021
19. EBRAINS - Ultrahigh resolution 3D cytoarchitectonic map of Area hOc3v (LingG) created by a Deep-Learning assisted workflow. https://search.kg.ebrains.eu/instances/Dataset/f746514d-b79a-48e2-9c07-39f7c62459cf. Accessed 6 Mar 2021
20. EBRAINS - Ultrahigh resolution 3D cytoarchitectonic map of Area hOc5 (LOC) created by a Deep-Learning assisted workflow. https://search.kg.ebrains.eu/instances/Dataset/ea8fb74b-0ecc-4801-9522-b4c2cb2a2a5c. Accessed 6 Mar 2021
21. Krause, D., Thörnig, P.: JURECA: modular supercomputer at Jülich Supercomputing Centre. J. Large-Scale Res. Facil. JLSRF **4**, A132 (2018). https://doi.org/10.17815/jlsrf-4-121-1
22. Omidyeganeh, M., et al.: Non-linear registration of 1 μm histology sections into 3D 20 μm BigBrain space (2020)
23. Schober, M., Axer, M., Huysegoms, M., Schubert, N., Amunts, K., Dickscheid, T.: Morphing image masks for stacked histological sections using laplace's equation. In: Tolxdorff, T., Deserno, T.M., Handels, H., Meinzer, H.-P. (eds.) Bildverarbeitung für die Medizin 2016. I, pp. 146–151. Springer, Heidelberg (2016). https://doi.org/10.1007/978-3-662-49465-3_27
24. Lewiner, T., Lopes, H., Ilson Vieira, A.W., Tavares, G.: Efficient implementation of Marching Cubes' cases with topological guarantees. J. Graph. Tools **8**(2), 1–15 (2003)
25. Andrews, T.J., Halpern, S.D., Purves, D.: Correlated size variations in human visual cortex, lateral geniculate nucleus, and optic tract. J. Neurosci. **17**(8), 2859–2868 (1997). https://doi.org/10.1523/jneurosci.17-08-02859.1997
26. Chen, X., Wang, F., Fernandez, E., Roelfsema, P.R.: Shape perception via a high-channel-count neuroprosthesis in monkey visual cortex. Science **370**(6521), 1191–1196 (2020). https://doi.org/10.1126/science.abd7435
27. Mirochnik, R.M., Pezaris, J.S.: Contemporary approaches to visual prostheses. Mil. Med. Res. **6**(1), 1–9 (2019). https://doi.org/10.1186/s40779-019-0206-9
28. Nuzzi, R., Dallorto, L., Rolle, T.: Changes of visual pathway and brain connectivity in glaucoma: a systematic review. Front. Neurosci. **12**(May), 363 (2018). https://doi.org/10.3389/fnins.2018.00363
29. Sepulcre, J., et al.: Contribution of white matter lesions to gray matter atrophy in multiple sclerosis evidence from voxel-based analysis of T1 lesions in the visual pathway. Arch. Neurol. **66**(2), 173–179 (2009). https://doi.org/10.1001/archneurol.2008.562
30. Schirner, M., et al.: Brain modelling as a service: the virtual brain on EBRAINS, February 2021. http://arxiv.org/abs/2102.05888. Accessed 1 June 2021

Brain Modelling and Simulation

Computational Modelling of Cerebellar Magnetic Stimulation: The Effect of Washout

Alberto Antonietti[1,2]([✉]) [iD], Claudia Casellato[2] [iD], Egidio D'Angelo[2,3] [iD], and Alessandra Pedrocchi[1] [iD]

[1] Politecnico di Milano, Piazza Leonardo da Vinci 32, 20133 Milan, Italy
alberto.antonietti@polimi.it
[2] University of Pavia, Via Forlanini 6, 27100 Pavia, Italy
[3] IRCCS Mondino Foundation, Via Mondino 2, 27100 Pavia, Italy

Abstract. Nowadays, clinicians have multiple tools that they can use to stimulate the brain, by means of electric or magnetic fields that can interfere with the bio-electrical behaviour of neurons. However, it is still unclear which are the neural mechanisms that are involved and how the external stimulation changes the neural responses at network-level. In this paper, we have exploited the simulations carried out using a spiking neural network model, which reconstructed the cerebellar system, to shed light on the underlying mechanisms of cerebellar Transcranial Magnetic Stimulation affecting specific task behaviour. Namely, two computational studies have been merged and compared. The two studies employed a very similar experimental protocol: a first session of Pavlovian associative conditioning, the administration of the TMS (effective or sham), a washout period, and a second session of Pavlovian associative conditioning. In one study, the washout period between the two sessions was long (1 week), while the other study foresaw a very short washout (15 min). Computational models suggested a mechanistic explanation for the TMS effect on the cerebellum. In this work, we have found that the duration of the washout strongly changes the modification of plasticity mechanisms in the cerebellar network, then reflected in the learning behaviour.

Keywords: Brain simulation · Cerebellum · Spiking Neural Networks · TMS · Neurostimulation

1 Cerebellar Transcranial Magnetic Stimulation

Transcranial magnetic stimulation (TMS) is a noninvasive technique that can be used to study, diagnose, or treat neural pathologies. A coil induces a magnetic

This project has been developed within the CerebNEST HBP Partnering Project and has received funding from the European Unions Horizon 2020 Framework Programme for Research and Innovation under Grant Agreement No. 785907 (Human Brain Project SGA2).

K. Amunts et al. (Eds.): BrainComp 2019, LNCS 12339, pp. 35–46, 2021.
https://doi.org/10.1007/978-3-030-82427-3_3

field that generates an electric field in the brain tissue. The electric field directly interferes with nervous system functions by changing the electrical behaviour of neurons.

Among the different protocols that are available for TMS, continuous theta-burst stimulation is usually delivered to influence long-term plasticity changes. The stimulation protocol can consist of pulse bursts 50 Hz repeated every 200 ms, given in a continuous train lasting tens of seconds. The stimulation intensity is calibrated using the active motor threshold, defined as the lowest intensity stably evoking motor-evoked potentials. Common values for the stimulation amplitudes for theta-burst TMS range between 0.5 and 0.7 kV, generating a peak magnetic field of ~1 T reaching a depth of 20–30 mm from the scalp surface [13].

Cerebellar TMS foresees the administration of the stimulation over one cerebellar hemisphere or the cerebellar vermis, and it can be used during cerebellar-driven protocols to interfere with the learning processes at neural level. It has been shown that cerebellar TMS stimulation influences the learning processes, but the underlying mechanisms are still unconfirmed [7,10,12,16].

In order to better understand the effects of cerebellar TMS, both experimental and computational approaches have been used in the last years.

2   Experimental Protocols

Monaco and colleagues [13,14] have employed TMS stimulation on human participants between two sessions of eyeblink conditioning protocol (EBC), a temporal associative task in which the subject learns, thanks to cerebellar plasticity, the precise timing associations between two stimuli. In EBC, the participant learns the association between a neutral conditioned stimulus (e.g., a sound) and a following unconditioned stimulus, eliciting an eyeblink (e.g., an electric shock near the eye). Initially, subjects respond with a reflexive eyelid closure, following the unconditioned stimulus. Along with learning of this association, participants start to express a Conditioned Response (CR), anticipating the unconditioned stimulus.

The two EBC studies [13,14] have common features, such as the presence of two consecutive sessions of EBC ($session_1$ and $session_2$), each one composed of 6 blocks of acquisition, where two stimuli were provided to the subject, and one block of extinction, where only one stimulus was provided to the subject. In the acquisition phase, the subject learns the timing association between the two stimuli, thus exhibiting an increasing percentage of correct CRs. In the extinction phase, the subject unlearns the association between the two stimuli, since the second one no more follows the first one. In both studies, an effective or a sham cerebellar TMS stimulation was administered at the end of the first session. The studies aimed at investigating the behavioural differences between the TMS and the control (sham) groups in the second session.

There are some minor discrepancies between the two experimental protocols (see Table 1), but the most important one is the washout period between the first and the second session of EBC: a long one (i.e., 1 week) in Monaco et al. 2014 [13], and a short one (i.e., 15 min) in Monaco et al. 2018 [14].

Table 1. Details of the two EBC experimental protocols

Property	Monaco et al. 2014	Monaco et al. 2018
Number of subjects for each group	11	12
Number of groups	2	3
Stimulated hemisphere	Right	Right or left
Number of trials per block	10	11
Inter-stimulus interval	600 ms	400 ms
Washout period	1 week	15 min

In both experimental datasets, changes in the learning and unlearning trajectories of CRs between the TMS and the control groups were observed. Namely, with a long washout, the TMS group showed impairment in the extinction phase of $session_2$ (from block 6 to block 7), where the unlearning resulted in being slowed down (Fig. 1.A). With a short washout, the TMS groups (right or left stimulated hemisphere) showed a less effective relearning phase at the beginning of acquisition (block 1 of $session_2$) and, again, a slowed down unlearning during the extinction phase (Fig. 1.B).

Overall, the findings from both experimental studies suggested that TMS can impair memory consolidation processes in the cerebellum, possibly by interfering with memory transfer from the cerebellar cortex to deeper structures. However, due to the noninvasive nature of TMS investigation, it was possible to only speculate about the putative mechanisms underlying the behavioural differences. To have a greater insight about the neural processes involved by the TMS, a computational approach was used in two previous works [1,3].

3   Computational Modelling

Historically, computational models of the brain have been widely used to acquire new knowledge that cannot be obtained from physiological studies and abstract theories. These models proved to be a powerful tool that can support the other approaches in tackling the complex problem of understanding how the brain works. Spiking Neural Networks (SNNs) have been used to mimic the neural organization, employing single units (i.e., the neurons) organized and connected similarly to the relative biological structures [4,9].

Recently, a detailed spiking neural network model of the cerebellar microcircuit proved able to reproduce multiple cerebellar-driven tasks [5], among which the EBC paradigm [2]. Having been validated, the SNN model was challenged to fit the two experimental datasets recorded by Monaco and colleagues from human subjects [13,14], with a long [1] or a short washout [3]. In both studies, the SNN model was able to capture the specific alterations in the second EBC session caused by TMS interference. Indeed, TMS affected motor response evolution along task repetitions, and we inferred the underpinning plasticity changes over the whole network.

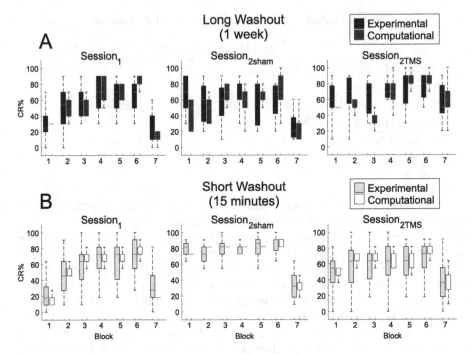

Fig. 1. CR percentages in experimental and modelling studies. A) Box-plots of CR percentages along the seven blocks of the EBC protocol with a long washout (1 week) between $session_1$ and $session_2$. Left panel: $session_1$, Central panel: $session_2$ with sham TMS, Right panel: $session_2$ with effective TMS. Boxes represent the upper and lower quartiles, the whiskers identify the range, and the red lines represent median values. Black boxes represent experimental data from [13] and blue boxes represent modelling data from [1] B) Box-plots of CR percentages along the seven blocks of the EBC protocol with a short washout (15 min) between $session_1$ and $session_2$. Grey boxes represent experimental data from [14], and white boxes represent modelling data from [3]. (Color figure online)

The SNN cerebellar microcircuit was populated with leaky Integrate&Fire neurons, distinguishing between different neural groups. Mossy Fibers (MFs), the input neurons of the system, encode the first (conditioned) stimulus. In fact, it has been shown that these neurons encode the state of the system (e.g., the presence of a certain sound). Granular Cells (GrCs) represent in a sparse way the input from the MFs. Inferior Olive neurons (IOs), the other input to the system, encode the second (unconditioned) stimulus, since this neural population is active in presence of pain. Purkinje Cells (PCs) integrate the sparse information coming from the GrCs through the Parallel Fibers (PFs), while Deep Cerebellar Nuclei (DCNs), the only output of the cerebellar microcomplex, activate the motor response (i.e., the anticipatory CR). While the network structure and connectivity are the same in the two computational studies (Fig. 2), the number of neurons for each population is different, as reported in Table 2, since the SNN used in Antonietti et al. 2018 is three-times larger than the one used in Antonietti et al. 2016. Both studies used EDLUT simulator environment to perform the neural simulations [17].

The connectivity between the different neural populations follows the same rules. MFs send projections to the GrCs, each GrC receives input from 4 MFs; IOs send one-to-one teaching connections to PCs; DCNs receive both excitatory

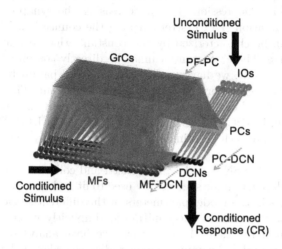

Fig. 2. Spiking Neural Network model used to simulate the cerebellar circuit. Both computational studies [1,3] used the same network architecture, but with a different number of neurons for each neural population (see Table 2). Circles represent neurons and lines represent synaptic connections. Plasticity sites are marked by orange labels. The first (conditioned) stimulus is encoded by MFs, while the second (unconditioned) is encoded by IOs. The activity of DCNs is the network output and generates CRs. (Color figure online)

Table 2. Number of neurons and synapses of the SNNs cerebellar models

Neural population	Antonietti et al. 2016	Antonietti et al. 2018
MFs	100	300
GrCs	2000	6000
IOs	12	36
PCs	12	36
DCNs	6	18
Synaptic connection		
MF-GrC (static)	8000	24000
PF-PC (plastic)	19164	172806
IO-PC (static)	12	36
MF-DCN (plastic)	600	5400
PC-DCN (plastic)	12	36

inputs directly from MFs and inhibitory synapses from PCs. The SNN models has three plasticity sites, at cortical level (PF-PC) and at nuclear level, between MF-DCN and PC-DCN, all based on different kinds of Spike-Timing Dependent Plasticity (STDP) [6,11]. PF-PC plasticity is modulated by IO activity, MF-DCN by PC activity, while PC-DCN is a standard unsupervised STDP learning, depending only on the difference between the pre- and post-synaptic firing times [8,15,18]. Each learning rule encompasses two different plasticity mechanisms: Long Term Depression (LTD), decreasing the synapse strength, and Long Term Potentiation (LTP), strengthening the connection. Therefore, each plasticity site can be characterized by two constants that regulate the amount of synaptic change. These constants cannot be directly computed from physiological data; as a result, we have treated those as free parameters of the SNN model, to be optimized according to the desired behaviour. The two computational studies employed evolutionary algorithms to identify the best six parameters (PF-PC LTP, PF-PC LTD, MF-DCN LTP, MF-DCN LTD, PC-DCN LTP, and PC-DCN LTD) in each experimental condition ($session_1$, $session_{2sham}$, and $session_{2TMS}$).

Employing realistic SNN models, Antonietti and colleagues have shown how closed-loop simulations can be successfully used to fit real experimental datasets. Thus, the changes in the model parameters in the different sessions of the protocol unveil how microcircuit mechanisms let implicitly emerge healthy and altered behavioural functions. In this work, we have analyzed the data generated by experimental and computational studies, in order to clarify the role of the washout period, the main difference between the two datasets.

4   Comparative Analysis

The elements analyzed in the present study are the learning and unlearning trajectories (i.e., the variation in CR percentage between blocks) and the values of LTP and LTD parameters at the three plasticity sites that yielded to different behaviours in the simulations.

The two computational studies have already demonstrated that the behavioural response generated by the model in each block was a good representation of the experimental recordings. Figure 1 shows that the CRs generated by the model (blue boxes in Panel A, white boxes in Panel B) were comparable with the experimental results (black boxes in Panel A, grey boxes in Panel B). The degree of variability of the experimental data was higher than the computational studies, but a certain degree of variability was maintained. The variability in the results generated by SNN models was due to the fact that multiple combinations of LTP and LTD parameters have been considered. In fact, the evolutionary algorithm identified a family of optimal parameter combinations, leading to similar performances.

For the short washout protocol, two distinct TMS groups were identified, one receiving a stimulation of the left cerebellar hemisphere, the other one receiving the stimulation on the right hemisphere. Since there were no significant differences between the CRs recorded from the two groups, in the present study, the results of both groups have been merged in a single TMS group, then compared to the sham group. In this way, we can make a direct comparison between the two studies, considering only two groups: sham vs TMS.

We focused our analysis on the two salient phases that were changed in $session_2$ for the TMS group with respect to the sham group. Namely, the fast acquisition (from zero to block 1, Fig. 3.A) and the extinction (from block 6 to block 7, Fig. 3.B). After a prolonged washout, the percentage of CRs acquired in the first block did not differ between the sham and the TMS groups. On the other hand, TMS slowed down the fast learning phase when a short washout interleaved the two EBC sessions (73% sham, 54.5% TMS, Fig. 3.A).

Conversely, the TMS administration interfered with the extinction phase after both long and short washouts. In fact, with a long washout the TMS group decreased the percentage of CRs of only −30% [−40 −10], while the sham group unlearnt faster −50% [−60 −40]. The same behaviour was observed with a short washout, where the extinction rate was −36% [−55 −27] in TMS group and −55% [−64 −45] in the sham group.

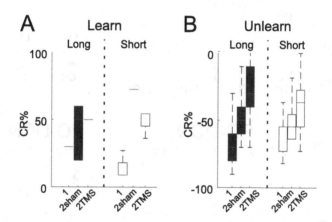

Fig. 3. Comparison of learning and unlearning rates in $session_1$, $session_{2sham}$, and $session_{2TMS}$. A) Fast learning rates, i.e., increase in CRs in the first acquisition block with long (left) or short (right) washouts. B) Unlearn rates, i.e. decrease in CRs from the last block of extinction (block 6) to the extinction (block 7). Boxes represent the upper and lower quartiles, the whiskers identify the range, and the red lines represent median values. Blue boxes represent modelling data from [1] and white boxes represent modelling data from [3]. (Color figure online)

Summarizing, the TMS affected both the fast acquisition and the extinction only with a short washout, while it impacted only the extinction phase with a long washout. We have then analyzed the LTP and LTD parameters of the SNN distributed plasticity that generated this different behaviour.

Figure 4 illustrates the overall variations of LTP and LTD parameters for the cortical plasticity (PF-PC, Panel A) and the nuclear plasticities (MF-DCN,

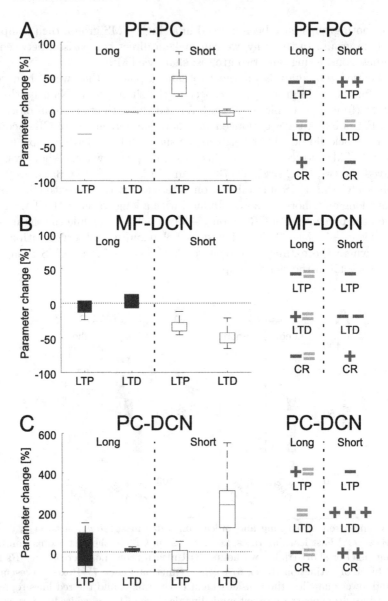

Fig. 4. Changes for LTP and LTD Parameter at the Three Different Plasticity Sites: A) PF-PC, B) MF-DCN, and C) PC-DCN. The left column represents box-plots of the parameter change in $session_2$ for the TMS group with respect to the parameter values for the sham group. Boxes represent the upper and lower quartiles, the whiskers identify the range, and the red lines represent median values. Blue boxes represent modelling data from [1] and white boxes represent modelling data from [3]. The right column presents a synthesis of the parameter changes (LTP and LTD) and the overall effect on the CR generation. Plus/minus symbols indicate qualitatively the amount of increase/decrease of the parameter in the TMS group or an increase/decrease in CR percentage generation. Equal symbols indicate negligible changes. (Color figure online)

Panel B, and PC-DCN, Panel C). The left column reports the percentage variation of the LTP and LTD parameters in the TMS group with respect to the sham group. An increased LTP parameter implicates a stronger potentiation of the synapses, while an increased LTD parameter entails a stronger weakening. The right column summarizes the combined effect of LTP and LTD changes and their effect on the CR generation process, that can be favoured or hindered.

Considering the PF-PC plasticity, it is possible to observe that while the LTD constant was not influenced by the TMS stimulation, the LTP parameter was decreased with a long washout and increased with a short one. This cause an increased and a decreased generation of CRs in the long and short washout case, respectively.

Considering the nuclear plasticities, the changes were limited for both LTP and LTD parameters in the long washout case. On the other hand, the changes were evident for the short washout case, where the variations of LTP and LTD parameters moved in favour of a generation of CRs. In fact, the LTD of the excitatory MF-DCN synapses was decreased, while the LTD of the inhibitory PC-DCN synapses was strongly increased. As a result, more excitatory inputs from the MFs and a weaker inhibition from the PCs increased the firing rate of DCN, thus generating more CRs.

5   Discussion and Conclusions

The analysis of LTP and LTD parameters showed that changes in behaviour with short and long washout are due to different rate in the rules driving synaptic modifications.

In particular, it can be observed that the administration of TMS followed by a prolonged washout caused a significant modification of the cortical plasticity only, with minor involvement of nuclear plasticities. Besides, the decrease of the PF-PC LTP parameter was in favour of a generation of CRs, therefore the fast acquisition in $session_{2TMS}$ was not impaired since the SNN expressed a high number of CRs, but this change impacted the extinction phase, where suppression of CRs was required.

In the case of a short washout, the parameters changed in a completely different way. First of all, it has been observed an involvement of both the cortical and the nuclear sites. While the cortical plasticity expressed a higher value of LTP, thus hindering CRs generation, the LTP and LTD constants of nuclear plasticities moved toward values that promoted CRs. As a matter of fact, the cortical and the nuclear mechanisms worked in opposite directions. This is the reason why, in the short washout case, both the learning and unlearning phases were impaired. The learning phase was slowed down by a weaker PF-PC response, while the reduced extinction was due to a higher DCN activity caused by the nuclear plasticities.

We can, therefore, conclude that the duration of the washout after the TMS administration is a crucial variable that can change the reorganization of plasticity and neural dynamics in the cerebellum. Since the TMS induces an electrical field in the most superficial areas of the tissue, the cortical plasticity is the one primarily involved, as reflected by major changes concerning its LTP mechanisms (increasing or decreasing the potentiation effectiveness). However, if sufficient recovery time is granted, the TMS effect is limited to the cerebellar cortex and does not interfere with deeper systems (i.e., nuclear plasticities) and memory transfer. Viceversa, if the inter-session pause after TMS perturbation is shortened, the cortical impairment in the acquisition phase triggers a compensatory effect of the nuclear plasticities, that try to favour CRs generation, but on a longer time-scale. Then, the nuclear compensation becomes an obstacle during the extinction phase.

It is important to highlight that the effect of TMS is more evident for the short washout, both in the experimental and computational studies. In fact, $session_{2sham}$ and $session_{2TMS}$ experimental data for the long washout protocol show high variability during the acquisition blocks. At the same time, the computational model fit those blocks with less fidelity. The second EBC session after a long washout suffers from the interference of the neural activity and synaptic changes that naturally happen during one week of participants' life, where external stimuli and internal processes can disrupt or modify cerebellar memory formation and consolidation.

This work carried out a retrospective analysis and a comparison of TMS-perturbed EBC paradigms that present some differences both from the experimental protocol (see Sect. 2, Table 1) and the related computational studies (see Sect. 3, Table 2). However, we believe that this comparative analysis provides a summary of the mechanistic explanations that can be derived from the interpretation of the SNN model parameters, highlighting the effects of the washout period in studies that foresee the administration of (cerebellar) TMS on human participants.

Data Availability. Datasets and Codes to reproduce the findings and figures reported in this paper is publicly available at Harvard Dataverse (DOI: 10.7910/DVN/9HPEV4).

References

1. Antonietti, A., Casellato, C., D'Angelo, E., Pedrocchi, A.: Model-driven analysis of eyeblink classical conditioning reveals the underlying structure of cerebellar plasticity and neuronal activity. IEEE Trans. Neural Netw. Learn. Syst. **28**, 2748–2762 (2016). https://doi.org/10.1109/TNNLS.2016.2598190
2. Antonietti, A., et al.: Spiking neural network with distributed plasticity reproduces cerebellar learning in eye blink conditioning paradigms. IEEE Trans. Biomed. Eng. **63**(1), 210–219 (2016). https://doi.org/10.1109/TBME.2015.2485301
3. Antonietti, A., Monaco, J., D'Angelo, E., Pedrocchi, A., Casellato, C.: Dynamic redistribution of plasticity in a cerebellar spiking neural network reproducing an associative learning task perturbed by TMS. Int. J. Neural Syst. **28**(09), 1850020 (2018). https://doi.org/10.1142/S012906571850020X
4. Brette, R., et al.: Simulation of networks of spiking neurons: a review of tools and strategies. J. Comput. Neurosci. **23**(3), 349–398 (2007). https://doi.org/10.1007/s10827-007-0038-6

5. Casellato, C., et al.: Adaptive robotic control driven by a versatile spiking cerebellar network. PLoS ONE **9**(11), e112265 (2014). https://doi.org/10.1371/journal.pone. 0112265

6. D'Angelo, E., et al.: Modeling the cerebellar microcircuit: new strategies for a long-standing issue. Front. Cell. Neurosci. **10**(July), 176 (2016). https://doi.org/ 10.3389/fncel.2016.00176

7. Galea, J.M., Albert, N.B., Ditye, T., Miall, C.: Disruption of the dorsolateral prefrontal cortex facilitates the consolidation of procedural skills. J. Cogn. Neurosci. **22**(6), 1158–1164 (2010). https://doi.org/10.1162/jocn.2009.21259

8. Geminiani, A., Casellato, C., Antonietti, A., D'Angelo, E., Pedrocchi, A.: A multiple-plasticity spiking neural network embedded in a closed-loop control system to model cerebellar pathologies. Int. J. Neural Syst. **28**, 1750017 (2017). https://doi.org/10.1142/S0129065717500174

9. Ghosh-Dastidar, S., Adeli, H.: A new supervised learning algorithm for multiple spiking neural networks with application in epilepsy and seizure detection. Neural Netw. **22**(10), 1419–1431 (2009). https://doi.org/10.1016/J.NEUNET.2009.04.003

10. Hadipour-Niktarash, A., Lee, C.K., Desmond, J.E., Shadmehr, R.: Impairment of retention but not acquisition of a visuomotor skill through time-dependent disruption of primary motor cortex. J. Neurosci. **27**(49), 13413–13419 (2007). https:// doi.org/10.1523/JNEUROSCI.2570-07.2007

11. Luque, N.R., Garrido, J.A., Naveros, F., Carrillo, R.R., D'Angelo, E., Ros, E.: Distributed cerebellar motor learning: a spike-timing-dependent plasticity model. Front. Comput. Neurosci. **10**(March), 1–22 (2016). https://doi.org/10.3389/fncom. 2016.00017

12. Miall, C., King, D.: State estimation in the cerebellum. Cerebellum **7**(4), 572–576 (2008). https://doi.org/10.1007/s12311-008-0072-6

13. Monaco, J., Casellato, C., Koch, G., D'Angelo, E.: Cerebellar theta burst stimulation dissociates memory components in eyeblink classical conditioning. Eur. J. Neurosci. **40**(July), 1–8 (2014). https://doi.org/10.1111/ejn.12700

14. Monaco, J., Rocchi, L., Ginatempo, F., D'Angelo, E., Rothwell, J.C.: Cerebellar theta-burst stimulation impairs memory consolidation in eyeblink classical conditioning. Neural Plast. **2018**, 1–8 (2018). https://doi.org/10.1155/2018/6856475

15. Ojeda, I.B., Tolu, S., Pacheco, M., Christensen, D.J., Lund, H.H.: A combination of machine learning and cerebellar-like neural networks for the motor control and motor learning of the fable modular robot. J. Robot. Netw. Artif. Life **4**, 62–66 (2017). https://doi.org/10.2991/jrnal.2017.4.1.14

16. Richardson, A.G., et al.: Disruption of primary motor cortex before learning impairs memory of movement dynamics. J. Neurosci. **26**(48), 12466–12470 (2006). https://doi.org/10.1523/JNEUROSCI.1139-06.2006

17. Ros, E., Carrillo, R.R., Ortigosa, E.M., Barbour, B., Agís, R.: Event-driven simulation scheme for spiking neural networks using lookup tables to characterize neuronal dynamics. Neural Comput. **18**(12), 2959–2993 (2006). https://doi.org/ 10.1162/neco.2006.18.12.2959

18. Tolu, S., Vanegas, M., Garrido, J.A., Luque, N.R., Ros, E.: Adaptive and predictive control of a simulated robot arm. Int. J. Neural Syst. **23**(3), 1350010 (2013). https://doi.org/10.1142/S012906571350010X

Usage and Scaling of an Open-Source Spiking Multi-Area Model of Monkey Cortex

Sacha J. van Albada[1,2](✉), Jari Pronold[1,3], Alexander van Meegen[1,2], and Markus Diesmann[1,4,5]

[1] Institute of Neuroscience and Medicine (INM-6), Institute for Advanced Simulation (IAS-6), and JARA Institute Brain Structure-Function Relationships (INM-10), Jülich Research Centre, Jülich, Germany
s.van.albada@fz-juelich.de
[2] Institute of Zoology, Faculty of Mathematics and Natural Sciences, University of Cologne, Cologne, Germany
[3] RWTH Aachen University, Aachen, Germany
[4] Department of Physics, Faculty 1, RWTH Aachen University, Aachen, Germany
[5] Department of Psychiatry, Psychotherapy and Psychosomatics, School of Medicine, RWTH Aachen University, Aachen, Germany

Abstract. We are entering an age of 'big' computational neuroscience, in which neural network models are increasing in size and in numbers of underlying data sets. Consolidating the zoo of models into large-scale models simultaneously consistent with a wide range of data is only possible through the effort of large teams, which can be spread across multiple research institutions. To ensure that computational neuroscientists can build on each other's work, it is important to make models publicly available as well-documented code. This chapter describes such an open-source model, which relates the connectivity structure of all vision-related cortical areas of the macaque monkey with their resting-state dynamics. We give a brief overview of how to use the executable model specification, which employs NEST as simulation engine, and show its runtime scaling. The solutions found serve as an example for organizing the workflow of future models from the raw experimental data to the visualization of the results, expose the challenges, and give guidance for the construction of an ICT infrastructure for neuroscience.

Keywords: Computational neuroscience · Spiking neural networks · Primate cortex · Simulations · Strong scaling · Reproducibility · Reusability · Complexity barrier

1 Introduction

With the availability of ever more powerful supercomputers, simulation codes that can efficiently make use of these resources (e.g., [1]), and large, systematized data sets on brain architecture, connectivity, neuron properties, genetics,

© The Author(s) 2021
K. Amunts et al. (Eds.): BrainComp 2019, LNCS 12339, pp. 47–59, 2021.
https://doi.org/10.1007/978-3-030-82427-3_4

transcriptomics, and receptor densities [2–10], the time is ripe for creating large-scale models of brain circuitry and dynamics.

We recently published a spiking model of all vision-related areas of macaque cortex, relating the network structure to the multi-scale resting-state activity [11,12]. The model simultaneously accounts for the parallel spiking activity of populations of neurons and for the functional connectivity as measured with resting-state functional magnetic resonance imaging (fMRI). As a spiking network model with the full density of neurons and synapses in each local microcircuit, yet covering a large part of the cerebral cortex, it is unique in bringing together realistic microscopic and macroscopic activity.

Rather than as a finished product, the model is intended as a platform for further investigations and developments, for instance to study the origin of oscillations [13], to add function [14], or to go toward models of human cortex [15].

To support reuse and further developments by others we have made the entire executable workflow available, from anatomical data to analysis and visualization. Here we provide a brief summary of the model, followed by an overview over the workflow components, along with a few typical usage examples.

The model is implemented in NEST [16] and can be executed using a high-performance compute (HPC) cluster or supercomputer. We provide corresponding strong scaling results to give an indication of the necessary resources and optimal parallelization.

2   Overview of the Multi-Area Model

The multi-area model describes all 32 vision-related areas in one hemisphere of macaque cortex in the parcellation of Felleman and Van Essen [17]. Each area is represented by a layered spiking network model of a 1 mm^2 microcircuit [18], adjusted to the area- and layer-specific numbers of neurons and laminar thicknesses. Layers 2/3, 4, 5, and 6 each have an excitatory and an inhibitory population of integrate-and-fire neurons. To minimize downscaling distortions [19], the local circuits contain the full density of neurons and synapses. This brings the total size of the network to ~4 million neurons and ~24 billion synapses. All neurons receive an independent Poisson drive to represent the non-modeled parts of the brain.

The inter-area connectivity is based on axonal tracing data from the CoCo-Mac database on the existence and laminar patterns of connections [4], along with quantitative tracing data also indicating the numbers of source neurons in each area and their supragranular or infragranular location [22,23]. These data are complemented with statistical predictions ('predictive connectomics') to fill in the missing values, based on cortical architecture (neuron densities, laminar thicknesses) and inter-area distances [24]. Figure 1 shows the resulting connectivity at the level of areas, layers, and populations. A semi-analytical mean-field method adjusts the data-based connectivity slightly in order to bring the firing rates into biologically plausible ranges [25].

By increasing the synaptic strengths of the inter-area connections, slow activity fluctuations, present in experimental recordings but not in the isolated microcircuit, are reproduced. In particular, the system needs to be poised right below

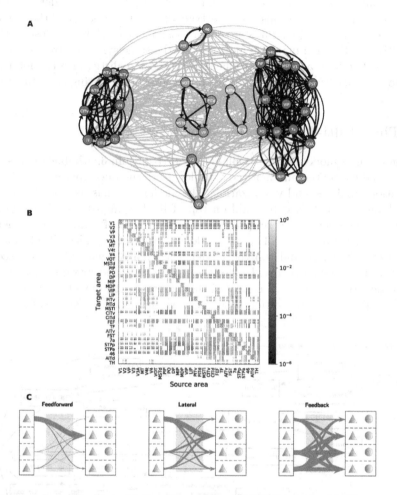

Fig. 1. Overview of the connectivity of the multi-area model as determined from anatomical data and predictive connectomics. **A** Area-level connectivity. The weighted and directed graph of the number of outgoing synapses per neuron (out-degrees) between each pair of areas is clustered using the map equation method [20]. Green, early visual areas; dark blue, ventral stream areas; purple, frontal areas; red, dorsal stream areas; light red, superior temporal polysensory areas; light blue, mixed cluster. Black arrows show within-cluster connections, gray arrows between-cluster connections. **B** Population-level connection probabilities (the probability of at least one synapse between a pair of neurons from the given populations). **C** Hierarchically resolved average laminar patterns of the numbers of incoming synapses per neuron (in-degrees). Hierarchical relationships are defined based on fractions of supragranular labeled neurons (SLN) from retrograde tracing experiments [21]: feedforward, $SLN > 0.65$; lateral, $0.35 \leq SLN \leq 0.65$; feedback, $SLN < 0.35$. The connections emanate from excitatory neurons and are sent to both excitatory and inhibitory neurons. For further details see [11].

an instability between a low-activity and a high-activity state in order to capture the experimental observations. The spectrum of the fluctuations and the distribution of single-neuron spike rates in primary visual cortex (V1) are close to those in lightly anesthetized macaque monkeys. At the same synaptic strengths where the parallel spiking activity of V1 neurons is most realistic, also the inter-area functional connectivity is most similar to macaque fMRI resting-state functional connectivity.

3   The Multi-Area Model Workflow

The multi-area model code is available via https://inm-6.github.io/multi-area-model/ and covers the full digitized workflow from the raw experimental data to simulation, analysis, and visualization. The model can thus be cloned to obtain a local version, or forked to build on top of it. The implementation language is Python, the open-source scripting language the field of computational neuroscience has agreed on [26]. The online documentation provides all information needed to instantiate and run the model. The tool Snakemake [27] is used to specify the interdependencies between all the scripts and execute them in the right order to reproduce the figures of the papers on the model's anatomy [11], dynamics [12], and stabilization based on mean-field theory [25] (see Fig. 2).

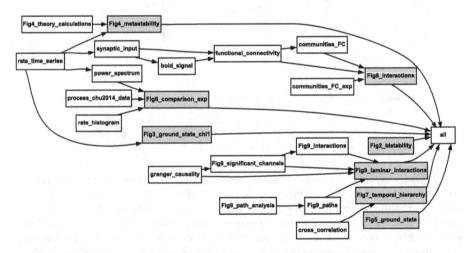

Fig. 2. Visualization of a Snakemake workflow. The interdependencies between the scripts reproducing the figures in [12], visualized as a directed acyclic graph. The label of a node corresponds to the name of the script.

Furthermore, if one of the files in the workflow is adjusted, Snakemake enables executing only that file and the ones that depend on it anew. A tutorial video (https://www.youtube.com/watch?v=YsH3BcyZBcU) gives a brief overview of the model, explains the structure of the code, and shows how to run a basic simulation.

4   Example Usage

One main property delivered by the multi-area model is the population-, layer-, and area-specific connectivity for all vision-related areas in one hemisphere of macaque cortex. We here describe how to obtain the two available versions of this connectivity: 1) based directly on the anatomical data plus predictive connectomics that fills in the missing values; 2) after slight adjustments in the connectivity in order to arrive at plausible firing rates in the model. We also refer to this procedure as 'stabilization' because obtaining plausible activity entails enhancing the size of the basin of attraction of the low-activity state, i.e., increasing its global stability. An example how to use the mean-field method developed in [25] for this purpose is provided in the model repository: figures/SchueckerSchmidt2017/stabilization.py. The method adjusts the number of incoming connections per neuron (in-degree). The script exports the adjusted matrix of all in-degrees as a NumPy [28] file; to have the matrix properly annotated one can instantiate the `MultiAreaModel` class with the exported matrix specified in the connection parameters as `K_stable`. Afterwards, one can access the connectivity using the instantiation M of the `MultiAreaModel` class: M.K for the in-degrees or `M.synapses` for the total number of synapses between each pair of populations. To obtain the connectivity without stabilization, it is sufficient to instantiate the `MultiAreaModel` class without specifying `K_stable`.

Performing a simulation of the full multi-area model requires a significant amount of compute resources. To allow for smaller simulations, it is possible to simulate only a subset of the areas. In this case, the non-simulated areas can be replaced by Poisson processes with a specified rate. To this end, the options `replace_non_simulated_areas` and `replace_cc_input_source` in `connection_params` have to be set to 'het_poisson_stat' and the path to a JSON file containing the rates of the non-simulated areas. Lastly, the simulated areas have to be specified as a list, for instance

```
sim_params['areas_simulated'] = ['V1', 'V2'],
```

before the `MultiAreaModel` class is instantiated. A simple example how to deploy a simulation is given in run_example_fullscale.py; the effect of replacing areas by Poisson processes is shown in Fig. 3.

5   Strong Scaling

The limiting factor dictating the necessary compute resources for simulating the multi-area model is the available memory. Approximately 1 TB is needed for instantiating the network alone. To ensure sufficient memory for the model, the simulation has to be distributed across multiple nodes.

We simulated the model using NEST 2.14 [29] on the JURECA supercomputer in Jülich, which provides 1872 compute nodes equipped with two Intel Xeon E5-2680 v3 Haswell CPUs per node. Each CPU has 12 cores running at 2.5 GHz. The standard compute node provides 128 GB of memory of which 96

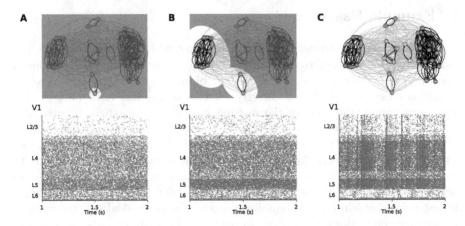

Fig. 3. Simulating subsets of the multi-area model. Bottom panels, spiking activity of excitatory (blue) and inhibitory (red) neurons in all layers of area V1 where in **A** and **B** a subset of areas is replaced by Poisson processes. Top panels, sketches visualizing which areas were simulated (white spotlights); the colors therein correspond to different clusters: lower visual (green), ventral stream (dark blue), dorsal stream (red), superior temporal polysensory (light red), mixed cluster (light blue), and frontal (purple). If all areas besides V1 are replaced by Poisson processes (**A**), the activity displays no temporal structure. Simulating a subset of ten areas (**B**) slightly increases the activity but does not give rise to a temporal structure, either. Only the simulation of the full model (**C**) produces a clear temporal structure in the activity. Parameters identical to [12, Fig. 5].

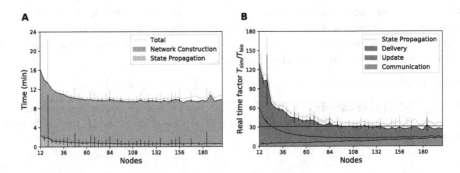

Fig. 4. Strong scaling of the multi-area model. The contributions of different phases to the total simulation time and state propagation for 12 to 200 compute nodes for 1 s of biological time. Each data point consists of three random network realizations, with error bar showing the standard deviation of measurements. **A** The main contributions to the total time are network construction and state propagation. **B** The state propagation is dominated by three phases: the communication, update, and spike delivery phase. Adding more compute resources while keeping network size the same (strong scaling) decreases the latter two but increases the absolute and relative contribution of the communication phase. The combined contributions are minimized at a real-time factor of 31 (black horizontal line). Parameters identical to [12, Fig. 5].

GB are guaranteed to be available for the running application. Thus, on this machine, the multi-area model needs at least 11 nodes.

Having established the minimal hardware requirements, we are interested in the runtime of the simulation depending on the compute resources. We quantify the proximity of the time required for state propagation to biological real time by the real-time factor $T_{\mathrm{sim}}/T_{\mathrm{bio}}$. Carrying out a strong scaling experiment, the problem size stays fixed and we increase the number of compute nodes from 12 to 200, thus reducing the load per node. In our simulations we use 6 MPI processes per node and 4 threads per MPI process, as we found this hybrid parallelization to perform better than other combinations of threading and MPI parallelism (data not shown). In particular during the construction phase, hybrid parallelization outperformed pure threading by a large margin. The threads are pinned to the cores and jemalloc is used as a memory allocator ([30], see [31] for the relevance of the allocator for NEST). In each run, we simulate 10 s of biological time.

In Fig. 4**A** the total runtime and its main contributions, network construction and state propagation, are shown. The contribution of state propagation is averaged to 1 s of biological time. The main share of the time is taken up by network construction. During this phase the neurons and synapses are created and connected, while during state propagation the dynamics of the model is simulated. The time spent in the former phase is fixed, as it is independent of the specified biological time, whereas the time spent propagating the state depends on the specified biological time and the state of the network. Depending on the initial conditions and the random Poisson input, the network exhibits higher or lower activity, affecting the time spent propagating the state. Hence, the ratio of both phases should not be taken at face value. In some cases, longer simulations are of interest, increasing the relevance of the time spent propagating the state. Thus, it is interesting to know how different components of the state propagation algorithm contribute to this phase.

The three main phases during state propagation are: update of neuronal states, communication between MPI processes, and delivery of spikes to the target neurons within each target MPI process. Figure 4**B** shows the contributions of these phases to the real-time factor. Adding more compute resources brings down the contributions of the update and delivery phases and increases the time consumption of communication. Especially the delivery of spikes is heavily dependent on the network activity. At 160 nodes, a real-time factor of 31 is achieved (mean spike rate 14.1 spikes/s). This slowdown compared to real time enables researchers to study the dynamics of the multi-area model over sufficiently long periods, for example in detailed correlation analyses, but systematic investigations of plasticity and learning would still profit from further progress.

In order to test the influence of the communication rate on the time required for state propagation, we carried out a simulation of a two-population balanced random network [32] which has been used in previous publications on neuronal network simulation technology [1,31,33–36]. We use the same parameters as in [1], but replace connections governed by spike-timing dependent plasticity by static connections. In addition we set the numbers of neurons and synapses to match those in the multi-area model (resulting mean spike rate 12.9 spikes/s). The communication interval is determined by the minimum delay, as the spikes can be buffered over the duration of this delay while maintaining causality [37]. The multi-area model has a minimum delay of 0.1 ms, whereas the balanced random network has a uniform delay of 1.5 ms, so that communication occurs 15 times less often. Using 160 nodes and the same configurations as before, we find a real-time factor of 17. Here, 80% of the time is spent delivering the spikes to the target neurons locally on each process, whereas only 1% of the time is spent on MPI communication. Forcing the two-population model to communicate in 0.1 ms intervals by adding a synapse of corresponding delay and zero weight indeed requires the same absolute time for MPI communication as in the multi-area model. The real-time factor increases to 34, significantly larger than for the multi-area model. The increase is entirely due to a longer spike delivery phase. How the efficiency of spike delivery is determined by the network activity remains to be answered by future investigations. Possibly relevant factors are the wide distribution of spike rates in the multi-area model compared to the narrow one in the two-population model, and the different synchronization patterns of neuronal activity in the two models. In summary, less frequent MPI communication shifts the bottleneck to another software component while almost halving the total runtime. This opens up the possibility of speeding up the simulation even more through optimized algorithms for spike delivery on each target process.

6   Conclusions

The usefulness of large-scale data-driven brain models is often questioned [38–40], as their high complexity limits ready insights into mechanisms underlying their dynamics, large numbers of parameters and a lack of testing of models with new data may lead to overfitting and poor generalization, and function does not emerge magically by putting the microscopic building blocks together. However, this argument can also be turned around. It seems that in recent years the complexity of the majority of models and thereby their scope of explained brain functions is not increasing anymore. One reason is that elegant publications on minimal models explaining a single phenomenon are often also end points in that they have no explanatory power beyond their immediate scope. It remains unclear how the proposed mechanisms interact with other mechanisms realized in the same brain structure, and how such models can be used as building blocks for larger models giving a more complete picture of brain function. The powerful approach of minimal models from physics needs to be integrated with the systems perspective of biology. To achieve models able to make accurate predictions for a broad range of questions, the zoo of available models of individual brain regions and hypothesized mechanisms needs to be consolidated into large-scale models tested on numerous benchmarks on multiple scales [41]. Having an accurate, if complex, model of the brain that generates reliable predictions enables *in silico* experiments, for instance to predict treatment outcomes for neurological conditions, potentially even for individual subjects [42]. Furthermore, combining the bottom-up, data-driven approach with a top-down, functional approach allows models to be equipped with information processing capabilities. Creating such accurate, integrative models will require overcoming the complexity barrier computational neuroscience is facing. Without progress in the software tools supporting collaborative model development and the expressive digital representation of models and the required workflows, reproducibility and reusability cannot be maintained for more complex models.

On the technical side, simulation codes like NEST have matured to generic simulation engines for a wide range of models. Recent developments in the simulation technology of NEST have considerably sped up the state propagation and reduced the memory footprint [1] of large-scale network models. The rapid state propagation causes the network construction phase to take up a large fraction of the simulation time for simulations of short to medium duration. Furthermore, the fact that hybrid parallelization currently performs better than pure threading during the construction phase indicates that the code still spends time on the Python interpreter level and does not yet optimally make use of memory locality. For these reasons, speeding up network construction should be a focus of future work.

Our strong scaling results show that communication starts to dominate at an intermediate number of nodes, so that the further speed-up in the solution of the neuron equations cannot be fully exploited. Therefore, it would be desirable to develop methods for further limiting the time required for communication, for instance by distributing the neurons across the processes according to the modular structure of the neuronal network [43], as opposed to the current round-robin distribution. The longer delays between areas compared to within areas would then allow less frequent MPI communication, by buffering the spikes for the duration of the delay [37,43]. A major fraction of time is then spent in the spike delivery phase. Here an algorithm needs to transfer the spikes arriving at the compute node to their target neurons. It is our hope that in future a better understanding of the interplay between the intrinsically random access pattern and memory architecture will lead to more effective algorithms.

While the publication of the model code in a public repository enables downloading and executing the code, this requires setting up the simulation on the chosen HPC system, which may be nontrivial, and the HPC resources have to be available to the research group in the first place. Therefore, it would be desirable to link computing resources to the repository, enabling the code to be executed directly from it. The ICT infrastructure for neuroscience (EBRAINS) being created by the European Human Brain Project (HBP) has made first steps in this direction. A preliminary version of a digital workflow for the collaborative development of reproducible and reusable models was evaluated in [44]. Next to finding a concrete solution for the multi-area model at hand, the purpose of the present study was to extend the previous work and obtain a clearer picture of the requirements on collaborative model development and the digital representation of workflows. From the present perspective it seems effective not to reimplement the functionality of advanced code development platforms like GitHub in the HBP infrastructure but to build a bridge enabling execution of the models and storage of the results. An essential feature will be that the model repository remains portable by abstractions from any machine specific instructions and authorization information.

The microcircuit building block for this model [18] has found strong resonance in the computational neuroscience community, having already inspired multiple follow-up studies [45–52]. The multi-area model of monkey cortex developed by Schmidt et al. [11,12] and described here has a somewhat higher threshold for reuse, due to its greater complexity and specificity. Nevertheless, it has already been ported to a single GPU using connectivity generated on the fly each time a spike is triggered, thereby trading memory storage and retrieval for computation, which is possible in this case because the synapses are static [53]. We hope that the technologies presented here push the complexity barrier of neuroscience modeling a bit further out, such that the model will find a wide uptake and serve as a scaffold for generating an ever more complete and realistic picture of cortical structure, dynamics, and function.

Acknowledgments. Supported by the European Union's Horizon 2020 research and innovation program under HBP SGA1 (Grant Agreement No. 720270), the European Union's Horizon 2020 Framework Programme for Research and Innovation under Specific Grant Agreements No. 785907 and 945539 (Human Brain Project SGA2, SGA3), Priority Program 2041 (SPP 2041) "Computational Connectomics" of the German Research Foundation (DFG), and the Helmholtz Association Initiative and Networking Fund under project number SO-092 (Advanced Computing Architectures, ACA). Simulations on the JURECA supercomputer at the Jülich Supercomputing Centre were enabled by computation time grant JINB33.

References

1. Jordan, J., et al.: Extremely scalable spiking neuronal network simulation code: from laptops to exascale computers. Front. Neuroinform. **12**, 2 (2018)
2. van Albada, S.J., et al.: Bringing anatomical information into neuronal network models. arXiv preprint arXiv:2007.00031 (2020)
3. Zilles, K., et al.: Architectonics of the human cerebral cortex and transmitter receptor fingerprints: reconciling functional neuroanatomy and neurochemistry. Eur. Neuropsychopharmacol. **12**(6), 587–599 (2002)
4. Bakker, R., Thomas, W., Diesmann, M.: CoCoMac 2.0 and the future of tract-tracing databases. Front. Neuroinform. **6**, 30 (2012)
5. Reimann, M.W., King, J.G., Muller, E.B., Ramaswamy, S., Markram, H.: An algorithm to predict the connectome of neural microcircuits. Front. Comput. Neurosci. **9**, 120 (2015)
6. Erö, C., Gewaltig, M.O., Keller, D., Markram, H.: A cell atlas for the mouse brain. Front. Neuroinform. **12**, 84 (2018)
7. Tasic, B., et al.: Shared and distinct transcriptomic cell types across neocortical areas. Nature **563**, 72–78 (2018)
8. Gouwens, N.W., et al.: Classification of electrophysiological and morphological neuron types in the mouse visual cortex. Nat. Neurosci. **22**, 1182–1195 (2019)

9. Sugino, K., et al.: Mapping the transcriptional diversity of genetically and anatomically defined cell populations in the mouse brain. eLife **8**, e38619 (2019)
10. Winnubst, J., et al.: Reconstruction of 1,000 projection neurons reveals new cell types and organization of long-range connectivity in the mouse brain. Cell **179**(1), 268–281 (2019)
11. Schmidt, M., Bakker, R., Hilgetag, C.C., Diesmann, M., van Albada, S.J.: Multi-scale account of the network structure of macaque visual cortex. Brain Struct. Func. **223**(3), 1409–1435 (2018)
12. Schmidt, M., Bakker, R., Shen, K., Bezgin, G., Diesmann, M., van Albada, S.J.: A multi-scale layer-resolved spiking network model of resting-state dynamics in macaque visual cortical areas. PLoS Comput. Biol. **14**(10), e1006359 (2018)
13. Shimoura, R.O., Roque, A.C., Diesmann, M., van Albada, S.J.: Visual alpha generators in a spiking thalamocortical microcircuit model. In: 28th Annual Computational Neuroscience Meeting, P204 (2019)
14. Korcsak-Gorzo, A., van Meegen, A., Scherr, F., Subramoney, A., Maass, W., van Albada, S.J.: Learning-to-learn in data-based columnar models of visual cortex. In: Bernstein Conference 2019, W9 (2019)
15. Pronold, J., van Meegen, A., Bakker, R., Morales-Gregorio, A., van Albada, S.J.: Multi-area spiking network models of macaque and human cortices. In: NEST Conference 2019, p. 30 (2019)
16. Gewaltig, M.O., Diesmann, M.: NEST (NEural Simulation Tool). Scholarpedia **2**(4), 1430 (2007)
17. Felleman, D.J., Van Essen, D.C.: Distributed hierarchical processing in the primate cerebral cortex. Cereb. Cortex **1**, 1–47 (1991)
18. Potjans, T.C., Diesmann, M.: The cell-type specific cortical microcircuit: relating structure and activity in a full-scale spiking network model. Cereb. Cortex **24**(3), 785–806 (2014)
19. van Albada, S.J., Helias, M., Diesmann, M.: Scalability of asynchronous networks is limited by one-to-one mapping between effective connectivity and correlations. PLoS Comput. Biol. **11**(9), e1004490 (2015)
20. Rosvall, M., Axelsson, D., Bergstrom, C.T.: The map equation. Eur. Phys. J. Spec. Top. **178**(1), 13–23 (2009)
21. Markov, N.T., et al.: Anatomy of hierarchy: feedforward and feedback pathways in macaque visual cortex. J. Compar. Neurol. **522**(1), 225–259 (2014)
22. Markov, N.T., et al.: Weight consistency specifies regularities of macaque cortical networks. Cereb. Cortex **21**(6), 1254–1272 (2011)
23. Markov, N.T., et al.: A weighted and directed interareal connectivity matrix for macaque cerebral cortex. Cereb. Cortex **24**(1), 17–36 (2014)
24. Hilgetag, C.C., Beul, S.F., van Albada, S.J., Goulas, A.: An architectonic type principle integrates macroscopic cortico-cortical connections with intrinsic cortical circuits of the primate brain. Netw. Neurosci. **3**(4), 905–923 (2019)
25. Schuecker, J., Schmidt, M., van Albada, S.J., Diesmann, M., Helias, M.: Fundamental activity constraints lead to specific interpretations of the connectome. PLoS Comput. Biol. **13**(2), e1005179 (2017)
26. Muller, E., Bednar, J.A., Diesmann, M., Gewaltig, M.O., Hines, M., Davison, A.P.: Python in neuroscience. Front. Neuroinform. **9**, 11 (2015)
27. Köster, J., Rahmann, S.: Snakemake–a scalable bioinformatics workflow engine. Bioinformatics **28**(19), 2520–2522 (2012)
28. Harris, C.R., et al.: Array programming with NumPy. Nature **585**(7825), 357–362 (2020)

29. Peyser, A., et al.: NEST 2.14.0 (2017)
30. Evans, J.: Scalable memory allocation using jemalloc (2011). https://www. facebook.com/notes/facebook-engineering/scalable-memory-allocation-using-jemalloc/480222803919
31. Ippen, T., Eppler, J.M., Plesser, H.E., Diesmann, M.: Constructing neuronal network models in massively parallel environments. Front. Neuroinform. **11**, 30 (2017)
32. Brunel, N.: Dynamics of sparsely connected networks of excitatory and inhibitory spiking neurons. J. Comput. Neurosci. **8**(3), 183–208 (2000)
33. Helias, M., et al.: Supercomputers ready for use as discovery machines for neuroscience. Front. Neuroinform. **6**, 26 (2012)
34. Kunkel, S., et al.: Spiking network simulation code for petascale computers. Front. Neuroinform. **8**, 78 (2014)
35. Kunkel, S., Schenck, W.: The nest dry-run mode: efficient dynamic analysis of neuronal network simulation code. Front. Neuroinform. **11**, 40 (2017)
36. Kunkel, S., Potjans, T.C., Eppler, J.M., Plesser, H.E., Morrison, A., Diesmann, M.: Meeting the memory challenges of brain-scale simulation. Front. Neuroinform. **5**, 35 (2012)
37. Morrison, A., Mehring, C., Geisel, T., Aertsen, A., Diesmann, M.: Advancing the boundaries of high connectivity network simulation with distributed computing. Neural Comput. **17**(8), 1776–1801 (2005)
38. Eliasmith, C., Trujillo, O.: The use and abuse of large-scale brain models. Curr. Opin. Neurobiol. **25**, 1–6 (2014)
39. Frégnac, Y.: Big data and the industrialization of neuroscience: a safe roadmap for understanding the brain? Science **358**(6362), 470–477 (2017)
40. Bassett, D.S., Zurn, P., Gold, J.I.: On the nature and use of models in network neuroscience. Nat. Rev. Neurosci. **19**(9), 566–578 (2018)
41. Einevoll, G.T., et al.: The scientific case for brain simulations. Neuron **102**(4), 735–744 (2019)
42. Proix, T., Bartolomei, F., Guye, M., Jirsa, V.K.: Individual brain structure and modelling predict seizure propagation. Brain **140**(3), 641–654 (2017)
43. Pastorelli, E., et al.: Newblock scaling of a large-scale simulation of synchronous slow-wave and asynchronous awake-like activity of a cortical model with long-range interconnections. Front. Syst. Neurosci. **13**, 33 (2019)
44. Senk, J., et al.: A collaborative simulation-analysis workflow for computational neuroscience using HPC. In: Di Napoli, Edoardo, Hermanns, Marc-André., Iliev, Hristo, Lintermann, Andreas, Peyser, Alexander (eds.) JHPCS 2016. LNCS, vol. 10164, pp. 243–256. Springer, Cham (2017). https://doi.org/10.1007/978-3-319-53862-4_21
45. Lindén, H., et al.: Modeling the spatial reach of the LFP. Neuron **72**(5), 859–872 (2011)
46. Cain, N., Iyer, R., Koch, C., Mihalas, S.: The computational properties of a simplified cortical column model. PLoS Comput. Biol. **12**(9) (2016)
47. Hagen, E., et al.: Hybrid scheme for modeling local field potentials from point-neuron networks. Cereb. Cortex **26**(12), 4461–4496 (2016)
48. Schwalger, T., Deger, M., Gerstner, W.: Towards a theory of cortical columns: from spiking neurons to interacting neural populations of finite size. PLoS Comput. Biol. **13**(4), e1005507 (2017)
49. Shimoura, R.O., et al.: [Re] the cell-type specific cortical microcircuit: relating structure and activity in a full-scale spiking network model. ReScience **4**(1) (2018)

50. van Albada, S.J., et al.: Performance comparison of the digital neuromorphic hardware SpiNNaker and the neural network simulation software NEST for a full-scale cortical microcircuit model. Front. Neurosci. **12**, 291 (2018)
51. Knight, J.C., Nowotny, T.: GPUs outperform current HPC and neuromorphic solutions in terms of speed and energy when simulating a highly-connected cortical model. Front. Neurosci. **12**, 941 (2018)
52. Rhodes, O., et al.: Real-time cortical simulation on neuromorphic hardware. Phil. Trans. R. Soc. A **378**, 20190160 (2019)
53. Knight, J.C., Nowotny, T.: Larger GPU-accelerated brain simulations with procedural connectivity. Nat. Comput. Sci. **1**(2), 136–142 (2021)

Exascale Compute and Data Infrastructures for Neuroscience and Applications

Modular Supercomputing
for Neuroscience

Estela Suarez[1(✉)], Susanne Kunkel[2], Anne Küsters[3], Hans Ekkehard Plesser[2,4],
and Thomas Lippert[1,5]

[1] Jülich Supercomputing Centre (JSC) - Forschungszentrum Jülich GmbH,
Leo Brandt Strasse, 52428 Jülich, Germany
`e.suarez@fz-juelich.de`
[2] Faculty of Science and Technology, Norwegian University of Life Sciences (NMBU),
Ås, Norway
[3] Simulation Laboratory Neuroscience – Bernstein Facility for High Performance
Simulation and Data Analytics, Institute for Advanced Simulation,
Jülich Aachen Research Alliance, Jülich Research Center, Jülich, Germany
[4] Institute of Neuroscience and Medicine (INM-6), Jülich Research Center,
Jülich, Germany
[5] Frankfurt Institute for Advanced Studies (FIAS), Goethe-Universität Frankfurt,
Ruth-Moufang-Straße 1, 60438 Frankfurt am Main, Germany

Abstract. The precise simulation of the human brain requires coupling
different models in order to cover the different physiological and functional aspects of this extremely complex organ. Each of this brain models is implemented following specific mathematical and programming
approaches, potentially leading to diverging computational behaviour
and requirements. Such situation is the typical use case that can benefit
from the Modular Supercomputing Architecture (MSA), which organizes
heterogeneous computing resources at system level. This architecture
and its corresponding software environment enable to run each part of
an application or a workflow on the best suited hardware.

This paper presents the MSA concept covering current hardware and
software implementations, and describes how the neuroscientific workflow resulting of coupling the codes NEST and Arbor is being prepared
to exploit the MSA.

Keywords: Modular Supercomputing Architecture · MSA ·
Heterogeneous computer architectures · DEEP projects · Accelerators ·
Workflow · Neuroscience · Arbor · NEST

1 Introduction

Since the construction of the first cluster computer in the nineties [1], interconnecting a large number of commodity, general-purpose processors has become the
most popular approach to build High-Performance Computing (HPC) systems.
In recent years, these traditionally homogeneous clusters are being substituted
by heterogeneous configurations employing a variety of acceleration technologies.

© The Author(s) 2021
K. Amunts et al. (Eds.): BrainComp 2019, LNCS 12339, pp. 63–80, 2021.
https://doi.org/10.1007/978-3-030-82427-3_5

Computing devices are considered as *accelerators* when they have been designed to perform specific operations very fast. In principle, such definition would apply even to individual execution units within the CPU, such as tensor cores or advanced vector registers. However, in this paper we denote as accelerators only those out-of-package devices made of a very large number of relatively simple compute cores. Under this definition, the most frequently used example of an accelerator is a graphic processing unit (GPU). As their name says, GPUs were originally developed to very efficiently render and visualize graphics, but today their compute performance is also employed to perform floating point and tensor operations in all kinds of applications. Since accelerators are designed to execute auxiliary operations, they frequently depend on a CPU (considered as its host) to carry out important actions such as booting the accelerator and enabling it to communicate through the cluster-level high-speed network.

Accelerators rely on exploiting parallelism to compute, as their large number of compute cores/units are operated at relatively low frequencies. In consequence, they are able to achieve high peak-performances using less power than standard CPUs. Their energy efficiency – expressed through a high Flop/Watt ratio – is in fact the main reason for the success of accelerators in HPC. Clusters with accelerators are generally more energy-efficient than those without, and this difference becomes a major cost-factor in the operation of very large-scale platforms.

With regards to the system-level architectures of accelerated clusters, one can observe that typically one, two or more accelerators are integrated inside a node connected to a general purpose CPU via a PCIe interface. This node configuration is then multiplied several thousands of times, and the CPUs are interconnected with each other via some high-speed network. Recently, interconnection of the GPUs within the node has become possible, improving the ability to exchange data between them. In consequence the trend goes towards *GPU-islands* with four, six or even more GPUs per node. The negative consequence is a dramatic growth in compute power inside the accelerated-node, which is not compensated with a proportional increase in inter-node communication bandwidth. Therefore, though the scaling inside the node improves, the system-level scaling of codes is impeded by the imbalanced compute-to-communication capabilities between nodes.

The traditional programming model for node-level accelerated clusters is to run the main program in the host CPUs and offload compute-intensive kernels to the accelerators. For the large problems tackled by HPC, multi-node executions require exchanging data between the parts of the application running on the host and the accelerator. However, the static assignment of accelerators to CPUs within the node, added to the additional communication latencies that apply when inter-accelerator communication is executed through the host – what today is not always necessarily the case anymore –, limits the scalability and flexibility of this *node-level heterogeneous cluster* concept.

For example: an application running on a cluster with four GPUs per node might fully exploit the host CPUs but use only one of the GPUs attached to each one of them. In such case it will be hardly possible for other applications to use these free devices, as access needs to go through the CPU, which is busy.

In consequence, in this example almost 3/4 of the computation power of the system will remain idle. Obviously such situation would be avoided if the system is deployed with exactly the amount of accelerators per node required by the applications that will run on it. However, finding the right static configuration for all the users of the HPC system becomes impossible since the application portfolio is getting more and more diverse.

Today, the users of HPC systems employ codes ranging from high-scale, tightly coupled simulations, to high-performance data analytics (HPDA) and deep learning (DL). In fact, not only the applications are very different from each other, but even the workflows from individual users combine codes with very diverse requirements.

This is particularly the case in neuroscience, which aims at better understanding the behaviour of the possibly most complex organ in nature: the human brain. The huge scale spans (from nanometers to centimeters), the complexity of the involved physical and biological effects, and the tight interrelation between all of these aspects require the combination of various codes in order to reproduce the behaviour of the brain with some accuracy. All these codes present generally different requirements, making the overall usage scenario a natural candidate for using the a Modular Supercomputing Architecture (MSA).

The particular case addressed by this paper is the coupling of NEST and Arbor, two neuroscientific codes that can together bring a deep insight in the functions of the human brain. NEST simulations of large-scale networks of simple integrate-and-fire type model neurons are memory-bound due to the communication and memory accesses required to reproduce the exchange of neuronal signals, which dominate the total runtime [23]. Therefore, NEST runs best on general purpose clusters. On the other hand, Arbor simulates multi-compartment neurons with a very high computational cost per neuron and is therefore compute-bound, making it the ideal candidate to run on accelerators. The coupling of both codes could therefore profit from an MSA system in which CPU and accelerator resources can be reserved and allocated independently.

This paper explains the MSA and how a neuroscientific workflow combining the codes NEST and Arbor aims at employing it. Section 2 explains the architecture concept, while Sect. 3 and 4 describe current hardware platforms and their software environment. Section 5 describes the above-mentioned Nest-Arbor neuroscientific workflow, and the paper is summarized in Sect. 6.

2   The Modular Supercomputing Architecture (MSA)

The Modular Supercomputing Architecture (MSA) developed at the Jülich Supercomputing Centre (JSC) within the series of EU-funded *DEEP projects* [2, 3] aims at providing cost-effective computing capabilities fitting the needs of a wide range of computational sciences [4,5].

The MSA segregates heterogeneous resources and implements heterogeneity at system level, instead of node level (see Fig. 1). In its simplest configuration (the so-called cluster-booster approach [6]), a cluster made of general purpose CPUs

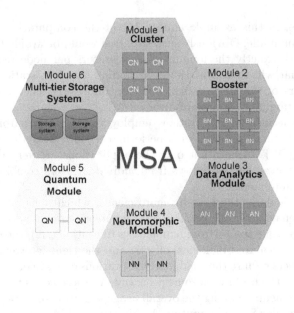

Fig. 1. Sketch of the modular supercomputing architecture. Note that this diagram reflects the general concept and does **not** represent any specific computer. Example modules: Cluster (*CN*: Cluster node), Booster (*BN*: Booster node), Data Analytics (*AN*: Analytics node), Neuromorphic (*NN*: Neuromorphic node), and Quantum (*QN*: Quantum node). For a schema of the MSA realization in the DEEP-EST prototype see Fig. 3, left.

is attached to a cluster of accelerators (the booster). In the latter accelerators are considered and operated as first-class computing devices. Furthermore, nodes on cluster and booster can be allocated independently and according to the needs of each application, so that no resources are blocked by allocating others.

In the first hardware realizations of the cluster-booster concept (e.g. JURECA, see Sect. 3.1), the booster used many-core processors that could boot and communicate through the system-level network without relying on host-CPUs. Fully autonomous accelerators are ideal for the MSA, as they enable scaling-up the cluster and the booster independently. In particular, the energy-efficient booster can be built at very large size (e.g. exascale), while the cluster is kept at a relatively small size to cover the needs of low-scaling parts of the applications without impacting on the overall power consumption of the system. Note that this is not possible in the traditional accelerated-node approach, where increasing the number of accelerators implies a proportional increase in the amount of general-purpose CPUs due to the static assignment between both.

Unfortunately, today's GPUs still rely on a host-CPU and cannot be operated autonomously. Still, the booster philosophy can be kept if one employs a low-power (and computationally weak) CPU, reducing its role to the orchestration and operation of the attached GPU(s). In this case, even if the number of CPUs increases when scaling-up the system, their contribution to the overall power consumption is very small. Another key goal of the booster is achieving a good intra-node and inter-node communication-to-computation balance. If the selected GPU is computationally very strong, it might be beneficial to keep a low number of them per node (eventually only one), in order to fully exploit all its bandwidth towards the network. These kind of considerations are crucial to achieve the goal of the booster: good system balance and energy-efficient scalability at system level.

Note, however, that the MSA is much more general than the cluster-booster concept, which is very much focused on matching the different concurrency levels in applications. In the same way as the cluster provides hardware support to run the low/medium scalable part of codes while the booster does the same for highly-scalable codes, some applications need different acceleration technologies and varying sizes of memory devices and capacities. The MSA aims at fulfilling the needs of very diverse application requirements by interconnecting a variety of compute modules. Each module is a multi-node system of potentially large side, designed with specific hardware configurations that target a part of the application portfolio.

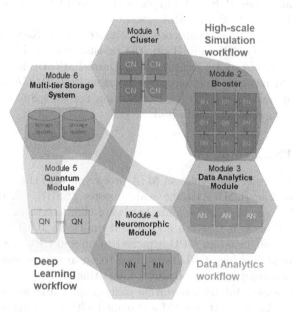

Fig. 2. Distribution of three different (hypothetical) workflows on an MSA system. See in Fig. 5 the mapping on the DEEP-EST prototype of the neuroscientific workflow matter of this paper.

One of the goals with MSA is to enable application developers to distribute their codes over a diversity of modules, such that each part of their workflows runs on the most suitable hardware (see Fig. 2). A further goal is to facilitate the adoption of new computing technologies in HPC. Therefore – though not yet implemented in existing platforms – the concept includes the option of integrating future technologies such as neuromorphic and quantum computing, providing seamless integration into a traditional HPC environment in order to enable their use in scientific workflows.

3   Current Hardware Platforms

Several MSA platforms have been deployed at JSC. Here two systems are described, showing how the architecture itself evolves with time employing the newest available technologies.

3.1   JURECA Cluster-Booster

In November 2017, with the deployment of its booster module, the JURECA cluster-booster system became the first modular supercomputer worldwide to be listed in the Top 500 list, reaching position 29 with the Linpack benchmark running over both partitions [7]. Both modules can obviously be operated separately, but what makes JURECA unique is that complex applications can also run across both, using it as one MSA system.

While the cluster uses multicore processors (Intel Xeon *Haswell*) and 100 Gb/s Mellanox (EDR) InfiniBand, the booster uses multi-core processors (Intel Xeon Phi *KNL*) and 100 Gb/s Intel Omni-Path. Bridging the two different high-speed network technologies is possible in JURECA through a customized development in the ParTec ParaStation Software Suite [8,9], which is continuously researched and optimized.

3.2   DEEP-EST Prototype

The DEEP-EST project has built an MSA-prototype with three compute modules: cluster module (CM), extreme scale booster (ESB), and data analytics module (DAM) – see Fig. 3. The main hardware characteristics of each module are detailed in Table 1. It is worth noting that, unlike in JURECA, the DEEP-EST booster is built using an GPU attached to an x86 CPU. As mentioned in Sect. 2, the role of this host-CPU is reduced to an auxiliary function and it is not intended to employ it for application computing.

The DAM module is intended to run the parts of applications dealing with large amounts of data. Therefore, the DAM is provided with very large memory capacity, combining both volatile and non-volatile technologies. Codes that can particularly profit from such capabilities are those performing data-analytics, or running machine learning or deep learning algorithms. The latter benefit also from acceleration devices containing tensor cores and support for mixed precision. For this reason, the DAM contains both NVIDIA GPUs and Intel Stratix10 FPGA units. With its variety of components the DAM is the module offering maximal flexibility. This comes at the prize of a higher energy consumption. However, since the DAM is only used for small-scale problems its node-number can be kept low.

Additional to the three compute modules, the DEEP-EST prototype contains two storage modules: the all-flash storage module (AFSM) and the hard-disk

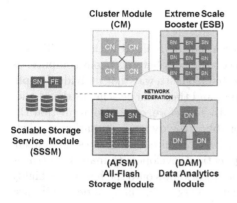

Fig. 3. Schema and picture of the DEEP-EST prototype at JSC (as of March 2021, fully installed).

Table 1. Key hardware features of the DEEP-EST MSA prototype.

DEEP-EST	CM	DAM	ESB
Time of deployment	2019	2019	2020
Node count	50	16	75
CPU type	Intel Xeon 6146	Intel Xeon 8260M	Intel Xeon 4215
CPU codename	Skylake	Cascade Lake	Cascade Lake
Cores @ frequency	12 @ 3.2 GHz	24 @ 2.4 GHz	8 @ 2.5 GHz
Accelerators per node	n.a	1× Nvidia V100 GPU	1× Nvidia V100 GPU
		1× Intel Stratix10 FPGA	
DDRA4 capacity	192 GB	384 GB	48 GB
HBM capacity	n.a	32 GB (GPU)	32 GB (GPU)
Node max. mem BW	256 GB/s	900 Gb/s (GPU)	900 GB/s (GPU)
NVM capacity	n.a	2/3 TB	n.a
NVMe/SATA SSD	512 GB	3 TB	250 GB
Power/node	500 W	1600 W	500 W
Cooling	warm-water	Air	Warm-water
Network technology	EDR-IB (100 Gb/s)	EXTOLL (100 Gb/s)	EDR-IB (100 Gb/s)
		Ethernet (40 Gb/s)	EXTOLL (100 Gb/s)
Topology	Fat-tree	Switched 2D-torus	tree/grid

based scalable storage module (SSSM), to enable fast I/O, run the file system and provide external storage capabilities.

All the compute and storage modules have been already installed and are up-and-running at JSC. The DEEP-EST prototype continues in operation beyond the end of the EU-funding time-frame and runs in near-production environment. It is being used for further development of the software stack and programming model of MSA systems in the DEEP-SEA project [2], as well as to run application tests to evaluate the benefits of its architecture and the functionality of its software stack.

4 Software Environment

The previous section showed how the MSA can be realized with very different hardware components. In fact, one could consider any heterogeneous computer as an MSA-system, as long as it can be operated in such a way that individual applications can run over various kinds of nodes, and these can be scheduled and allocated according to diverse application needs. Therefore, one could argue that the MSA is more a software infrastructure enabling the dynamic operation of a heterogeneous computer, rather than the hardware architecture of the system itself.

The MSA software stack enables application developers to map the intrinsic scalability patterns of their applications and workflows onto the hardware: highly parallel code parts run on the large-scale, energy-efficient booster, while less scalable code parts can profit from the high single-thread performance of the cluster, or from the high memory capacity of the data-analytics module. Users can freely decide how many nodes to use in each module, so that the highest application efficiency and system usage can be achieved [10].

4.1 Scheduling

The scheduling software used in the current MSA systems is SLURM [11]. Hardware heterogeneity is supported with SLURM's job-pack functionality, which provides semantics to express the amount of nodes to be reserved in each partition of an heterogeneous platform. The same annotation enables a user to run his/her workflow across nodes on different modules of an MSA system. However, in its current implementation SLURM statically reserves all nodes for the whole duration of the job, regardless of the fact that they are continuously used or not. For example, for a workflow performing pre-processing on the cluster and running then a long simulation on the booster, the nodes on the cluster will be kept reserved (and idle) until the simulation finishes in the booster. This is certainly not the wished behaviour on the MSA.

Extensions to the SLURM scheduler are therefore being implemented, aiming at reserving and releasing nodes for a job-pack when necessary. The DEEP-EST implementation relies on a new `---delay` switch, which can be used to inform the scheduler of the time-span between the start of one and the next job in a job-pack. Based on this information, the reservation of the second module can be started when it is actually needed, and not before. Further extensions to the scheduling and resource managing system for MSA are envisioned within the DEEP-SEA project.

4.2 Programming Environment

In order to facilitate portability, the MSA software stack aims at supporting the hardware complexity, while providing all the needed functionality and facing the application developers with the well-established interfaces and programming models that they know and use in other HPC systems. Therefore, the MSA programming paradigm is based on MPI. To support MSA-systems employing different network technologies in different modules (such as JURECA) a gateway protocol has been developed [12]. For application developers, this protocol is fully transparent and hidden behind the MPI library.

The simplest way of running an application on an MSA system is using only one module. Monolithic, highly scalable codes will actually likely run this way. On the other hand, codes that perform multi-physics or multi-scale simulations can run across compute modules and exchange data between them via MPI. This is the scenario displayed in Fig. 4, where an MPI application running on the cluster spawns part of its code to the booster.

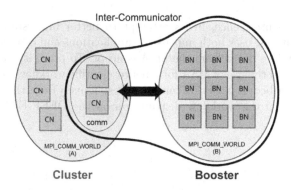

Fig. 4. Scheme of an MPI application running on the cluster and spawning part of its code to the booster.

MPI codes can be distributed over the MSA employing any of the collective instructions in the MPI standard allowing to connect two `MPI_Comm_World()` with each other. For instance, a subset of MPI tasks can collectively spawn a new `MPI_Comm_World()` to another module via the instruction `MPI_Comm_Spawn()`. Its inter-communicator connects the children to the parent processes and enables transferring data between them. Similarly, two `MPI_Comm_World()` running on different MSA modules can be connected with each other via the instruction `MPI_Connect()`. Furthermore, an `MPI_Comm_World()` can be split into two by using `MPI_Split()` and then send each one to a different module.

Arguably, splitting an MPI programm across modules is the most difficult way of using an MSA system. Distributing workflows is much simpler since one does not need to take care of the MPI communicators. In general, workflows use different codes used to execute different actions after (or in parallel) to each other. For example, a user may need to pre-process data before running a long simulation, then perform data-reduction, and ultimately visualize the final result. Running these codes on different modules consists simply on indicating to the scheduler on which nodes to execute each step. In the SLURM language a workflow is named a job-pack (see Sect. 4.1), and a set of SLURM instructions enables running each step on a different partition of module of an heterogeneous system.

Between the codes of a workflow data is currently transferred via the file-system, which means that it is written onto the external storage in one step, and then re-read in the next workflow-step. Taking into account the time and power consumed in such write-read operations, this approach is not necessarily the fastest, and certainly not the most scalable. Because of that, the DEEP-EST project has investigated the potential implementation and benefits of directly transferring data between workflow steps via MPI. The data can reside directly at the node-memories or be stored in new kind of network-attached memory devices [13].

5   Neuroscience Workflow on MSA

Computational neuroscience, in its attempt to better understand the human brain via simulations, uses both multi-scale applications and complex workflows, and should therefore profit from the MSA concept. To prove it, the DEEP-EST project has studied the use of MSA for a neuroscientific workflow in which NEST and Arbor (described in Sects. 5.1 and 5.2, respectively) are the main components. A schema of the workflow distribution on the DEEP-EST prototype is given in Fig. 5.

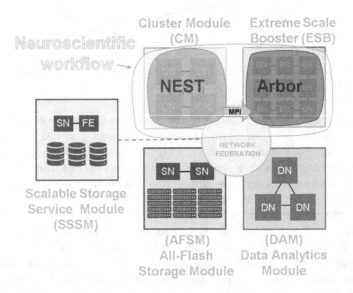

Fig. 5. Distribution of the neuroscientific workflow (NEST, Arbor) on the architecture of the DEEP-EST prototype.

Brain function involves the interaction of neurons located in different brain areas. Therefore, spiking neural network models representing multiple brain areas are becoming more and more popular in Computational Neuroscience. The multi-area model [14] is an early brain-scale model at the resolution of single neurons that incorporates experimental data defining the connections between neurons, called synapses. It comprises approximately four million highly simplified model neurons and on average 6000 incoming synapses per neuron. Recording all neuronal activity – called spikes – for the entire duration of a simulation could easily reach the terabyte data-volume range. Interpreting such data in a meaningful way is even more challenging, also because experimental techniques currently can only record spike activity of a small proportion of neurons in a brain area, limiting the experimental data available for comparison to simulation results.

Neuroscientists therefore also record mesoscale signals such as local field potentials (LFP): A single micro-electrode or an array of micro-electrodes is inserted into the brain tissue in order to record the electrical activity, especially input currents, of all neurons in a volume roughly 1 mm in diameter. Due to the use of highly simplified point neurons in, e.g., the multi-area model [14], LFP signals cannot be obtained directly from simulations of that or similar models.

The Python package LFPy[1] enables the calculation of local field potentials by driving simulations of uncoupled compartmental neuron models by the spike output of point neuron network models [16]. This multi-scale simulation thus allows for the comparison of LFP signals from brain-scale network models to experimental data. As the simulation of brain-scale point neuron networks and uncoupled compartmental neuron models create very different computational loads, the prediction of LFPs from brain-scale models presents an important neuroscience application for MSA systems such as the DEEP-EST prototype (see Sect. 3.2).

With this target neuroscience application in mind we have investigated the limits to NEST-Arbor co-simulation on the DEEP-EST prototype. Figure 6 illustrates the concept, while Sect. 5.1 and Sect. 5.2 describe the involved simulators NEST[2] and Arbor[3], respectively. The overall runtime of the multi-scale simulation depends on the individual runtimes of the simulators and the latency of the frequent collective MPI communication between CM and ESB.

5.1 NEST

NEST is a simulator for spiking neural network models that focuses on the dynamics, size and structure of neural systems. In such networks neuron models are typically simple: they do not account for any neuronal morphology and the dynamics is governed by a small number of coupled differential equations, which in some cases can even be exactly integrated [17]. This enables the simulation of large-scale networks, where each compute node hosts many neurons and their incoming synapses. As in biologically realistic models of the cortex each neuron connects to a few thousand other neurons, an inherent bottleneck of the simulation of such networks is the frequent communication of neuronal signals (spikes) between compute nodes and the delivery of the spikes to their local targets.

Large-scale neural network simulations with NEST make use of a hybrid parallelization scheme combining MPI and OpenMP threads, where users typically

---

[1] lfpy.readthedocs.io; github.com/LFPy/LFPy.

[2] nest-simulator.org; nest-simulator.readthedocs.io; github.com/nest/nest-simulator.

[3] arbor.readthedocs.io; github.com/arbor-sim/arbor.

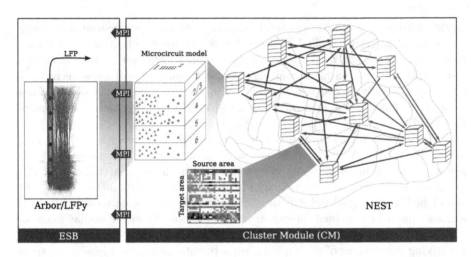

Fig. 6. Multi-scale simulation of a brain-scale network and concurrent calculation of
LFPs as the target neuroscience application on the DEEP-EST prototype, requiring
frequent transfer of neuronal activity data from the cluster module (CM) to the extreme
scale booster (ESB) through collective MPI communication. *Right:* Simulation of the
multi-area model [14] at single-neuron level resolution on the CM using NEST. Each
area is represented by an adapted microcircuit model [15] with area- and layer-specific
population sizes. Blue triangles and red dots in the magnified microcircuit-model illus-
tration indicate two different types of neurons and their varying population sizes across
layers. Connectivity between areas is based on experimental data and varies depending
on source and target area as indicated by the connectivity matrix. Adapted from Fig. 1
and Fig. 4D in [14]. *Left:* Simulation of one of the areas at sub-neuronal resolution using
Arbor on the ESB, and continuous calculation of LFPs using LFPy. Morphologies of
the multi-compartment neuron models are based on experimental data. Neurons are
not connected as all spike input is obtained from the multi-area model simulation on
CM. Adapted from Fig. 1 in [16]

define the network models and steer the simulations through the Python based
interface PyNEST [18]. A variety of neuron and synapse models are already
included in NEST but it also offers the possibility to define custom models
using the domain specific language NESTML [19]. NEST has an interface to
the Multi-Simulator Coordinator (MUSIC) [20], which enables multi-scale simulations. Besides, NEST's refactored recording infrastructure [21] facilitates the
definition of communication interfaces to other simulators such as Arbor. The
NEST code is open source. All contributions to the code-base undergo review
and are automatically tested by a continuous integration system running the
NEST testsuite [22].

NEST is a simulator with versatile applications: from interactive explorations
of small-scale networks on laptops to simulations of brain-scale networks on
supercomputers. With the introduction of the 5g simulation kernel [23,24] the
scalability of NEST has extended even further with respect to both runtime and
memory usage, see Fig. 5.1.

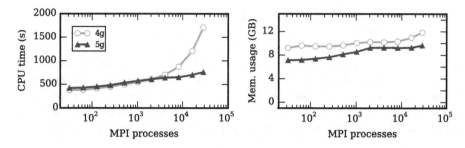

Fig. 7. Weak scaling of the NEST HPC benchmark on JUQUEEN for the current and the previous simulation kernel (NEST 5g and 4g, respectively). CPU time and memory usage per compute node for a network simulation for 1 s of biological real time, where each compute node hosts 18,000 neurons with 11,250 incoming synapses per neuron; 64% of all synapses have dynamically changing weights. Simulations were performed using 1 MPI process per compute node and 8 threads per MPI process. Adapted from Fig. 7 in [23].

The roadmap for the development of the simulation technology is defined by the NEST Initiative[4]. Current work comprises performance profiling and redesign of the algorithms underlying spike communication and spike delivery, and the development of more efficient ways of handling neuronal populations. This enables faster construction and simulation of highly structured networks such as the multi-area model (Fig. 7).

5.2 Arbor

Arbor is a performance-portable library for simulation of large networks of morphologically-detailed neurons on modern high-performance computing systems [25,26]. Arbor simulates networks of spiking neurons, particularly multi-compartment neurons. In these networks, the interaction between cells is conveyed by spikes and gap junctions and the multi-compartment neurons are characterized by axonal delays, synaptic functions and cable trees. Each cell is modelled as a branching, one-dimensional electrical system with dynamics derived from the balance of transmembrane currents with axial currents that travel through the intracellular medium, and with ion channels and synapses represented by additional current sources. Arbor additionally models leaky integrate-and-fire cells and proxy spike sources.

The Arbor library is an active open source project, written in C++14 and CUDA using an open development model. It can scale from laptops to the largest HPC clusters using MPI. The on-node implementation is specialized for GPUs, vectorized multicore, and Intel KNL with a modular design for enabling extensibility to new computer architectures, and employs specific optimizations for these GPU and CPU implementations. The GPU is deployed for updating currents and integrating gating variables using an optimized parallel GPU solver for

---

[4] nest-initiative.org.

sparse matrices with an optimized memory layout and reduced memory access. In detail, the GPU solver uses fine grained parallelization with one dendrite branch per thread, and a cell distribution into CUDA blocks to avoid global synchronization. In the simulation setup work balancing per thread avoids idle threads by sorting all submatrices on a level in a block by size. To maximize the utilization of the GPU memory bandwidth the memory layout is optimized by storing data in an interleaved format for each branch. Memory read access is reduced by storing only one parent compartment for each branch (Fig. 8).

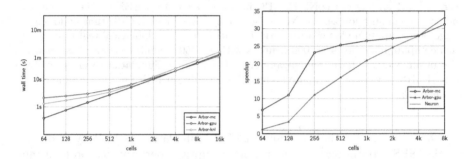

Fig. 8. Performance of Arbor. *Left*: Single node wall time of Arbor running on Piz Daint multicore, GPU and Tave KNL. *Right*: The single node speedup of Arbor running on Piz Daint multicore and GPU relative to NEURON on multicore. Adapted from Fig. 5 in [14].

By implementing the design goals of scalability, extensibility and performance portability, Arbor is an order of magnitude more efficient than existing simulation engines [25]. Arbor does this without sacrificing ease of use and flexibility. Arbor's single node speedup performance has been analyzed using a randomly connected network benchmark employing CSCS' Piz Daint multicore, GPU and KNL clusters. For more than 4,000 cells the GPU is utilized enough to run the benchmark more efficiently in terms of the wall time than on multicore or KNL (Fig. 5.2, left panel). Compared to NEURON [27], the most widely used software for general simulation of networks of multi-compartment cells, Arbor is 5–10× faster for fewer than 128 cells, and for more than 256 cells it is over 20× faster (Fig. 5.2, right panel).

Benchmarking and validation of Arbor and other simulators can be performed with the NSuite performance and validation testing suite[5] which is on-going work in Arbor development. Full support for the SONATA [28] model exchange format is under active development, as well as a Python API. Arbor will provide APIs for integration with other tools and simulators, including co-simulation with NEST. On a technical level a NEST-Arbor two-way coupled co-simulation imply some specific challenges, e.g., enabling injection of external spikes, as well as new initiation steps to align time delays and the number of external cells.

---

[5] nsuite.readthedocs.io; github.com/arbor-sim/nsuite.

6 Summary

The Modular Supercomputing Architecture (MSA) proposes a new philosophy for the integration and use of heterogeneous computing resources. Instead of regarding acceleration devices as intra-node entities and using them to speed-up very concrete kernels of the codes executed on general-purpose host-CPUs, the MSA strives for operating accelerators as first-class, autonomous compute elements. The MSA segregates the heterogeneous resources into individual modules, each one being a multi-node platform of potentially large size tailored to specific kinds or parts of applications. Each module can be sized differently, according to the energy efficiency of the hardware and the needs of the users. At the same time, applications and workflows can be distributed over different modules using the overarching MSA software environment, enabling each step to be executed on the best suited hardware.

The field of Computational Neuroscience is already preparing to employ the MSA approach, targeting the DEEP-EST prototype with a workflow that combines the codes NEST and Arbor. This multi-scale neuronal network simulation connects two types of neuronal simulations that are fundamentally different in computational load, memory access behaviour, and communication requirements.

A simulation of the multi-area model with NEST is not particularly computationally costly as it involves only the update of simple model neurons. In such large-scale network simulations it is rather the frequent and unpredictable exchange of neuronal signals that imposes stress on MPI communication and memory access, and thus dominates the total runtime. The cluster module is therefore best suited for this type of simulation.

For the Arbor simulation of multi-compartment neurons the computational costs per neuron are much higher than for a large-scale point-neuron network simulated with NEST. At the same time, the communication of spikes is of minor importance for the overall runtime of the Arbor simulation because it is much smaller in terms of number of neurons. In the planned application, the compartmental neurons are not even connected and communication of neuronal signals within Arbor is thus not required. Therefore, the Arbor simulation is more compute bound and can benefit from the GPUs of the DEEP-EST booster.

The installation of the DEEP-EST prototype has been completed with the deployment of its third and last module – the booster – in early 2020. NEST and Arbor have been adapted to run on the prototype, to show the benefits of executing an important neuroscientific workflow across the modules of an MSA platform. Adaptations to NEST and Arbor include the development of corresponding interfaces for spike exchange between the simulators, using MPI laying the groundwork for the neuroscience workflow (Sect. 5). Co-simulation benchmarks show that spiking network simulations with NEST running on the cluster module can be extended such that spikes generated in NEST drive compartmental neurons simulated with Arbor on the booster module without runtime penalty [29]. Moreover, the simulation time of NEST has been significantly reduced by optimizing the spike-delivery algorithm hiding memory fetch latency [29], which contributes to more efficient co-simulation. We consider the optimizations a generally useful contribution to large-scale network simulation as they are applicable to other simulators for pulse-coupled networks with high connection degrees.

Acknowledgements. S. Kunkel and H.E. Plesser thank the NEST developer community and Arbor developers for excellent collaboration. A. Küsters would like to thank Wouter Klijn and Ben Cumming for contributing to Sect. 5.2. With many thanks to the Arbor developers Nora Abi Akar, Benjamin Cumming, Felix Huber, Wouter Klijn, Alexander Peyser and Stuart Yates, as well as the SimLab Neuroscience at the Jülich Supercomputing Centre.

E. Suarez thanks all the institutions and individuals involved in the DEEP projects, who have contributed to the development of the MSA architecture, its prototype hardware implementations and its software environment.

Funding. This work has been partially funded by the European Union's Seventh Framework (FP7/20017-2013) and Horizon 2020 Framework Programmes for Research and Innovation under grant agreements 287530 (DEEP), 610476 (DEEP-ER), 754304 (DEEP-EST), 720270 (HBP SGA1), and 785907 (HBP SGA2). The present publication reflects only the authors' views. The European Commission is not liable for any use that might be made of the information contained therein.

The Arbor library is developed by the Swiss National Supercomputing Center and the Jülich Supercomputing Center under the auspices of the Human Brain Project, funded from the European Union's Horizon 2020 Framework Programme for Research and Innovation under the Specific Grant Agreement No. 720270 (Human Brain Project SGA1) and Specific Grant Agreement No. 785907 (Human Brain Project SGA2).

The authors also gratefully acknowledge the funding provided by the Helmholtz Programme *Supercomputing & Big Data* to realize the JURECA Cluster and Booster.

References

1. Becker, D.J., Sterling, T., Savarese, D., Dorband, J.E., Ranawak, U.A., Packer, C.V.: BEOWULF: a parallel workstation for scientific computation. In: Proceedings International Conference on Parallel Processing, vol. 95 (1995). http://www.phy.duke.edu/~rgb/brahma/Resources/beowulf/papers/ICPP95/icpp95.html
2. DEEP projects. http://www.deep-projects.eu
3. Eicker, N., Lippert, T., Moschny, T., Suarez, E.: The DEEP project - an alternative approach to heterogeneous cluster-computing in the many-core era. Concurrency Comput. Pract. Experience **28**, 2394–2411 (2016). https://doi.org/10.1002/cpe.3562
4. Suarez, E., Eicker, N., Lippert, T.: Supercomputer evolution at JSC. In: Proceedings NIC Symposium, vol. 49, p. 1–12 (2018). http://juser.fz-juelich.de/record/844072
5. Suarez, E., Eicker, N., Lippert, Th.: Modular supercomputing architecture: from idea to production. In: Vetter, J.S. (ed.) Contemporary High Performance Computing: From Petascale Toward Exascale, ch. 9, vol. 3, pp. 223–251. CRC Press (2019). https://juser.fz-juelich.de/record/862856
6. Eicker, N., Lippert, T.: An accelerated cluster-architecture for the exascale. In: PARS 2011, PARS-Mitteilungen, vol. 28, pp. 110–119 (2011)

7. Krause, D., Thörnig, P.: JURECA: modular supercomputer at Jülich supercomputing centre. J. Large-Scale Res. Facil. 4 (2018). https://doi.org/10.17815/jlsrf-4-121-1
8. ParaStationV5. http://www.par-tec.com/products/parastationv5.html
9. Clauss, C., et al.: Allocation-internal co-scheduling - interaction and orchestration of multiple concurrent MPI sessions. In: Advances in Parallel Computing, vol. 28, pp. 46–68. IOS Press BV (2017)
10. Kreuzer, A., et al.: Application Performance on a Cluster-Booster System. In: 2018 IEEE International Parallel and Distributed Processing Symposium Workshops (2018). https://doi.org/10.1109/IPDPSW.2018.00019
11. SLURM. https://slurm.schedmd.com/
12. Eicker, N., Galonska, A., Hauke, J., Nüssle, M.: Bridging the DEEP gap - implementation of an efficient forwarding protocol. Intel European Exascale Labs - Report 2013, vol. 1, pp. 34–41 (2014). http://juser.fz-juelich.de/record/171982
13. Schmidt, J.: Network attached memory, Chapter 4 of the Ph.D. thesis, Accelerating Checkpoint/Restart Application Performance in Large-Scale Systems with Network Attached Memory, Ruprecht-Karls University Heidelberg (Fakultät für Mathematik und Informatik). http://archiv.ub.uni-heidelberg.de/volltextserver/23800/1/dissertation_juri_schmidt_publish.pdf
14. Schmidt, M., Bakker, R., Hilgetag, C.C., Diesmann, M., van Albada, S.J.: Multiscale account of the network structure of macaque visual cortex. Brain Struct. Funct. 223(3), 1409–1435 (2017). https://doi.org/10.1007/s00429-017-1554-4
15. Potjans, T.C., Diesmann, M.: The cell-type specific cortical microcircuit: relating structure and activity in a full-scale spiking network model. Cereb. Cortex 24(3), 785–806 (2014). https://doi.org/10.1093/cercor/bhs358
16. Hagen, E., Næss, S., Ness, T.V., Einevoll, G.T.: Multimodal modeling of neural network activity: computing LFP, ECoG, EEG, and MEG signals with LFPy 2.0. Front. Neuroinform. 12, 92 (2018). https://doi.org/10.3389/fninf.2018.00092
17. Rotter, S., Diesmann, M.: Exact digital simulation of time-invariant linear systems with applications to neuronal modeling. Biol. Cybern. 81(5–6), 381–402 (1999). https://doi.org/10.1007/s004220050570
18. Eppler, J.M., Helias, M., Muller, E., Diesmann, M., Gewaltig, M.O.: PyNEST: a convenient interface to the NEST simulator. Front. Neuroinform. 2, 12 (2009) https://doi.org/10.3389/neuro.11.012.2008
19. Plotnikov, D., Rumpe, B., Blundell, I., Ippen, T., Eppler, J.M., Morrison, A.: NESTML: a modeling language for spiking neurons. In: Modellierung 2016, Lecture Notes in Informatics (LNI), pp. 93–108 (2016) https://doi.org/10.5281/zenodo.1412345
20. Djurfeldt, M., et al.: Run-time interoperability between neuronal network simulators based on the music framework. Neuroinformatics 8, 43–60 (2010). https://doi.org/10.1007/s12021-010-9064-z
21. Eppler, J.M., Peyser, A., Schenck, W.: The NESTio project - replacement data recording backend for NEST. In: NEST Conference (2017). juser.fz-juelich.de/record/842049
22. Eppler, J.M., Kupper, R., Plesser, H.E., Diesmann, M.: A testsuite for a neural simulation engine. Front. Neuroinform. Conference Abstract Neuroinformatics (2009). https://doi.org/10.3389/conf.neuro.11.2009.08.042
23. Jordan, J., et al.: Extremely scalable spiking neuronal network simulation code: from laptops to exascale computers. Front. Neuroinform. 12, 2 (2018). https://doi.org/10.3389/fninf.2018.00002

24. Linssen, C., et al.: NEST 2.16.0 Zenodo (2018). https://doi.org/10.5281/zenodo.1400175

25. Akar, N.A., et al.: Arbor – a morphologically-detailed neural network simulation library for contemporary high-performance computing architectures. In: Proceedings of 27th Euromicro International Conference on Parallel, Distributed and Network-Based Processing (PDP), pp. 274–282 (2019). https://doi.org/10.1109/EMPDP.2019.8671560

26. Akar, N.A., et al.: arbor-sim/arbor: Arbor Library v0.2 Zenodo (2019). https://doi.org/10.5281/zenodo.2583709

27. Carnevale, T.N., Hines, M.L.: The Neuron Book. Cambridge University Press (2006). https://doi.org/10.1017/CBO9780511541612

28. Dai, K., et al.: The SONATA data format for efficient description of large-scale network models. bioRxiv 625491 (2019, in preprint). https://doi.org/10.1101/625491

29. Kreuzer, A., et al.: DEEP-EST deliverable D1.5: final report on applications experience (2021). https://www.deep-projects.eu/project/deliverables.html

Fenix: Distributed e-Infrastructure Services for EBRAINS

Sadaf Alam[1], Javier Bartolome[2], Sanzio Bassini[3], Michele Carpene[3],
Mirko Cestari[3], Frederic Combeau[4], Sergi Girona[2], Stefano Gorini[1],
Giuseppe Fiameni[3], Björn Hagemeier[5], Andreas Herten[5], Nikoleta Kiapidou[2],
Wouter Klijn[5], Dorian Krause[5], Jacques-Charles Lafoucriere[4], Cerlane Leong[1],
Thomas Leibovici[4], Thomas Lippert[5], Colin McMurtrie[1], Pavel Mezentsev[5],
Anne Nahm[5], Boris Orth[5], Dirk Pleiter[5(✉)], Thomas Schulthess[1],
Benedikt von St. Vieth[5], Debora Testi[3], and Gilles Wiber[4]

[1] CSCS, Swiss National Supercomputing Centre, 6900 Lugano, Switzerland
[2] Barcelona Supercomputing Center, 08034 Barcelona, Spain
[3] CEA DAM, 91680 Bruyères-le-Châtel, France
[4] CINECA, 40033 Casalecchio di Reno, Italy
[5] JSC, Forschungszentrum Jülich, 52425 Jülich, Germany
pleiter@kth.se

Abstract. The Human Brain Project (HBP) (https://humanbrainpro ject.eu/) is a large-scale flagship project funded by the European Commission with the goal of establishing a research infrastructure for brain science. This research infrastructure is currently being realised and will be called EBRAINS (https://ebrains.eu/). The wide ranging EBRAINS services for the brain research communities require diverse access, processing and storage capabilities. As a result, it will strongly rely on e-infrastructure services. The HBP led to the creation of Fenix (https://fenix-ri.eu/), a collaboration of five European supercomputing centres, who are providing a set of federated e-infrastructure services to EBRAINS. The Fenix architecture has been designed to uniquely address the need for a wide spectrum of services, from high performance computing (HPC) to on-demand cloud technologies to identity and access federation, for facilitating ease of access and usage of distributed e-infrastructure resources. In this article we describe the underlying concepts for an audience of computational science end-users and developers of domain-specific applications, workflows and platforms services. To exemplify the use of Fenix, we will discuss selected use cases demonstrating how brain researchers can use the offered infrastructure services and describe how access to these resources can be obtained.

Keywords: Fenix · Human brain project · Distributed e-infrastructures

1 Introduction

Today, advances in addressing grand challenges depend on the ability of researchers coming from different geographic regions to effectively collaborate

K. Amunts et al. (Eds.): BrainComp 2019, LNCS 12339, pp. 81–89, 2021.
https://doi.org/10.1007/978-3-030-82427-3_6

and having flexible access to distributed e-infrastructure services. Fenix supports the former and provides the latter as it enables researchers, e.g., to collaborate on data curation, aggregation and sharing by providing federated storage sources as well as to use high-capability resources like High Performance Computing (HPC) systems.

The brain research community is a diverse community that applies a large variety of methods. It is thus not surprising that the requirements concerning e-infrastructure services are rather diverse. While some teams need massively-parallel HPC systems for large-scale simulations, others are producing extreme-scale data sets and employ advanced and potentially compute-intensive data analysis techniques. Given the size of the data sets, data analysis and making these data sets available to the wider community needs to be done in such a way that data transport can be avoided. This does not only help reducing costs or improving performance, in a number of cases this is mandatory given the involved amount of data. Yet other research teams perform computational and data analysis tasks requiring compute resources at smaller scale, but need to do this in an interactive manner.

Fenix is creating an infrastructure layer comprising services that are federated in a rather lightweight fashion. It is designed such that quite different types of compute services ranging from HPC to Cloud as well as different types of data repositories can be integrated. This initiative is realised by five European supercomputing centres, namely BSC in Spain, CEA in France, CINECA in Italy, CSCS in Switzerland, and JSC in Germany. Fenix is organised in such a way that other resource providers may join in the future.

This paper is organised as follows: In the next section we introduce the general concepts that led to the architecture of Fenix. In Sect. 3 we provide details on the Fenix services and discuss in Sect. 4 how EBRAINS services can make use of these. In Sect. 5 we describe how resources are allocated to users from HBP, before providing a summary and outlook in Sect. 6.

2   Fenix Concept

The current architecture of Fenix is based on the general consideration that a clear separation between an infrastructure service layer and a platform service layer is beneficial. Such a layered approach is commonly used for creating Cloud infrastructures (see, e.g., [2]), where the terms Infrastructure-as-a-Service (IaaS) and Platform-as-a-Service (PaaS) are widely used.

For Fenix we prefer to use the terms infrastructure service layer and platform service layer. The *platform service layer* encompasses all services that are specific for a given research domain. They are not necessarily useful for other domains or would require significant adaptations. A typical example are web-based portals, such as the EBRAINS Collaboratory[1]. While such portals are needed for almost any research infrastructure, their organisation is highly domain specific. The

---

[1] https://wiki.ebrains.eu.

infrastructure service layer includes a set of services that allow implementing these platform services and are sufficiently generic for being useful for different research communities. One example are machines for deploying any of the aforementioned portal services, which are typically offered in a virtualised environment. Using Virtual Machine (VM) technology allows for better exploitation of the hardware resources as a larger number of VMs, which typically only need the resources of a few CPU cores, can be deployed within a single physical machine.

The infrastructure services are organised such that they can be provided by multiple, geographically distributed resource providers. While this approach adds the complexity related to the federation of these services, the approach has a number of important benefits, which we will discuss below.

Most of the end-users are not expected to use the Fenix infrastructure services directly, but rather connect to the platform services that are deployed on top of these infrastructure services as shown in Fig. 1. For specialist users there is, however, the option to directly access the infrastructure services. An example are users performing simulations on massively-parallel HPC systems, who typically directly access these systems to compile and execute their simulation applications.

The layered approach has multiple benefits. In general, a layered approach and the resulting separation of concerns helps to manage complexity. From the perspective of the platform service providers, the abstraction of an infrastructure service layer can help improving sustainability and performance due to the distributed nature of the infrastructure service layer, involving multiple infrastructure resource providers. Resource providers can be replaced, for instance when funding conditions change, or the number of resource providers could be changed according to the needs of the platform service layer. Furthermore, platform service providers are enabled to improve on resilience by replicating their services over multiple sites. Another benefit of a distributed infrastructure is improved data locality. With a larger number of infrastructure resource providers, the probability that storage resources are available in geographic proximity of the data source increases. From the perspective of the infrastructure service providers, the layered approach has the benefit that it allows the consolidation of their service offerings when supporting multiple science communities. Finally, it creates opportunities for improving the utilisation of the offered hardware resources.

3   Fenix Compute and Data Services

In this section we provide an overview of the current service portfolio offered by Fenix, which was developed on the basis of an analysis of today's needs of the brain research communities. With other communities starting to use Fenix, the current portfolio of services is anticipated to change.

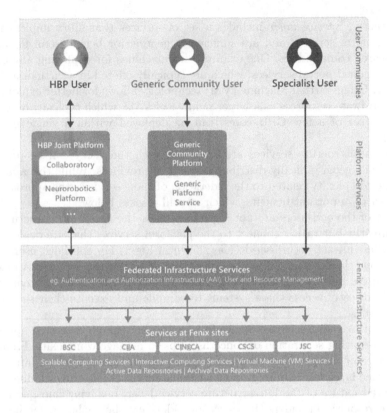

Fig. 1. Overview of the Fenix architecture as described in Sect. 2. Details on the infrastructure services are provided in Sect. 3.

The *Scalable Compute Services (SCC)* abstract large-scale computing resources. These are HPC systems with a larger number of compute nodes with 1–2 CPUs and possibly additional compute accelerators like GPUs. SCC services can be used for running highly parallel simulation applications, but are also suitable for data analysis tasks, involving extreme-scale data sets. SCC resources are managed by a batch queuing system, which schedules jobs such that hardware utilisation is optimised.

As an increasing demand for interactive access to compute resources is observed, Fenix introduces *Interactive Compute Services (IAC)* services. These allow end-users to obtain ad-hoc access to single compute nodes where interactive frameworks like Jupyter are offered. Typical usage scenarios are interactive analyses, visualisations, and steering of simulations running on SCC.

VM services offer access to on-demand virtualised machines. The prime use case for this service is the deployment of platform services running in a "24/7" mode, for instance web-based portal services.

To cope and comply with different and in parts incompatible needs and requirements, Fenix introduces two classes of data repositories. An *Archival Data*

Repository (ADR) is a storage system for long-term storage of data objects in a shareable manner. Such data repositories must therefore feature a standardised interface with easy to install clients and allow for federation. Mechanisms supporting flexible and fine-grained access control are another important feature. Fenix decided for the widely used Cloud object storage interface Swift[2].

Unlike an ARD, an *Active Data Repository (ADR)* is not a federated data repository that is relatively openly accessible from outside a data centre. An ACD is meant to be used for storing (copies of) private data sets and will typically offer $10 - 100\times$ more bandwidth as well as significantly lower latency. Such features are important for data repositories connected to SCC services. A typical implementation of an ACD is based on a parallel file system with a POSIX interface like Lustre[3] or Spectrum Scale[4].

Both types of data repositories will be connected through a *Data Mover* service that will allow to asynchronously copy or move data back and forth.

It is important to note that the different services have different security requirements. Some of them, like SCC, IAC and ACD, are realised in an *HPC environment* with tightly restricted access policies. VM services are deployed in a *Cloud environment* with an open connectivity. This will, e.g., allow users unknown to the data centre with weak or no credentials to connect to the platform services deployed on such resources. An ARD is connected to both environments and thus can serve as a bridge between both worlds. Other connections between services deployed in different environments are subject to negotiations to identify the right balance between the realisation of advanced workflows and security concerns.

Except for these restrictions, Fenix allows to combine the use of different services at different locations within a single project. This is a significant advantage compared to similar service offerings in Europe. Achieving this depends on the following prerequisites:

- All services must be integrated into a single Authentication and Authorisation Infrastructure (AAI) such that a user can connect with the same credentials to any service offered at any Fenix site.
- Resource management must be centralised such that both, a Fenix user as well as a Fenix resource provider, have an overview of the resources that are still available or have already been consumed.
- For coherent management of access control, a central service is needed that makes the necessary attributes available.

At the time of writing this article, a first version of the AAI is being put in operation, while the central resource management and attribute service, which is called FURMS, is still under development.

While the Fenix service portfolio is provided using general-purpose hardware technologies, the concept described in this section also allows for provisioning

---

[2] https://wiki.openstack.org/wiki/Swift.

[3] https://lustre.org/.

[4] https://www.ibm.com/products/spectrum-scale.

of infrastructure services, using special-purpose hardware solutions. Within the HBP there are, e.g., ongoing efforts to integrate neuromorphic computing services that are provided on the BrainScales [8] and SpiNNaker [4] systems at the Universities of Heidelberg and Manchester, respectively.

4   Selected EBRAINS Services

In this section we introduce a selected set of EBRAINS services and discuss how these can make use of Fenix services.

The EBRAINS *Brain Simulation Platform* comprises a suite of software tools and workflows for collaborative brain research that allow researchers to reconstruct and simulate detailed models of brain areas. This includes, e.g., simulators like NEST [5] and Neuron [7] as well as the neurophysiology data analysis tools package Elephant [3]. A simple workflow using Fenix services is shown in Fig. 2:

1. The input model data is assumed to be stored in ARD #1 and is copied to an ACD from where it is accessible to the SCC service.
2. The simulations are executed using the SCC service, which reads the input data from and writes the output data to the ACD.
3. After completing the simulation, the final data products can be published by copying the data to ARD #2.

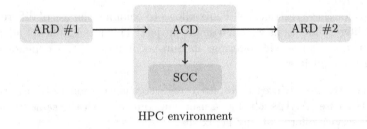

Fig. 2. Example for a brain simulation flow using Fenix services.

Next, we consider a more complex example related to the EBRAINS *Brain Atlases*. EBRAINS aims to provide access to a new generation of 3-dimensional reference atlases of the human and rodent brain, which are defined at different scales and modalities. These atlases are based on histological data obtained from brain images (see, e.g., [1]). A complex workflow is required to first analyse and interpret the images as well as to integrate this data (see, e.g., [6]) and to later make the Brain Atlas as well as primary and secondary data products available to others. A possible realisation of such a workflow is shown in Fig. 3, which can be mapped to Fenix services as follows:

1. The primary data products are generated in a lab and stored in an ARD.
2. SCC services allow processing of extreme-scale data sets as they occur in the case of images with a resolution of $\mathcal{O}(1\,\mu m)$, and facilitate the use of compute-intensive data analysis steps. To allow for fast access to the data, it will typically be staged from an ARD to an ACD. The resulting data products can be published after writing them into an ARD.
3. Multiple analysis steps using SCC services may follow.
4. Final data products may be explored interactively using IAC services.

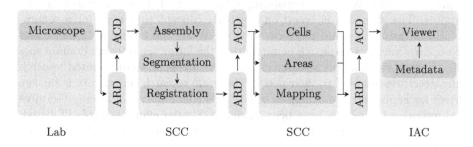

Lab   SCC   SCC   IAC

Fig. 3. Schematic view of a possible workflow for creating a Brain Atlas using Fenix services.

5 Resource Allocation

Part of the resources provided by Fenix are dedicated to HBP research and EBRAINS services as well as related research projects. A so-called programmatic access model allows to provide these resources to a research community (here the brain research community represented by HBP), with the latter being responsible for the allocation of the resources to projects proposed by researchers from that community.

The HBP allocates the resources based on a peer-review mechanism that follows principles established by PRACE[5]. Such a mechanism is widely used for making HPC resources available as it helps to ensure expensive resources being used for excellent science. The principles mandate, among other requirements, the peer-review process to be transparent and clear to all relevant stakeholders. Furthermore, the process must be fair such that all proposals are evaluated solely on merit and potential high impact on European and international science and economy.

Applicants interested in using Fenix resources for brain research can, at any time, submit a proposal. After a technical review by Fenix resource providers,

---

[5] https://prace-ri.eu/hpc-access/project-access/project-access-the-peer-review-proc ess/.

the EBRAINS Infrastructure Allocation Committee (IAC) is responsible for conducting or managing the scientific assessment in case of small- or large-scale resource requests, respectively. Based on the outcome of the review, the IAC can in the case of small-scale projects decide itself on whether to approve or reject a proposal. In the case of large-scale projects, the IAC prepares a decision-making proposal for the Directorate of the HBP.

6   Summary and Outlook

Fenix is an initiative that is realising a broad set of federated infrastructure services. The approach is based on a generic concept that aims for a separation of infrastructure and platform services. While the former are generic and of use for a variety of research communities, the latter are research domain specific. The approach allows research communities to establish distributed research infrastructures adapted to their needs. The brain research community is the key driver for Fenix and two examples of how this community can leverage services and resources from Fenix have been discussed. Similar efforts towards IT-based, distributed research infrastructures can, however, also be observed for other science communities.

The HBP has established mechanisms for allocating resources offered by Fenix, which is open for researchers from HBP but also for brain researchers at large. Other scientists can also apply for Fenix resources through regular calls for proposals managed by PRACE.

Acknowledgements. Funding for the work is received from the European Commission H2020 program under Specific Grant Agreement No. 800858 (ICEI). We would like to thank Timo Dickscheid (Forschungszentrum Jülich (FZJ), INM-1) for many discussions providing insight into the workflow for creating a brain atlas from brain imaging data.

References

1. Amunts, K., Zilles, K.: Architectonic mapping of the human brain beyond brodmann. Neuron **88** (2015) https://doi.org/10.1016/j.neuron.2015.12.001
2. Badger, L., Grance, T., Patt-Corner, R., Voas, J.: Cloud Computing Synopsis and Recommendations. Tech. rep, NIST (2012)
3. Denker, M., Yegenoglu, A., Grün, S.: Collaborative HPC-enabled workflows on the HBP collaboratory using the elephant framework. In: Neuroinformatics 2018, p. P19 (2018). https://doi.org/10.12751/incf.ni2018.0019
4. Furber, S.B., Galluppi, F., Temple, S., Plana, L.A.: The SpiNNaker project. Proc. IEEE **102**(5), 652–665 (2014). https://doi.org/10.1109/JPROC.2014.2304638
5. Gewaltig, M.O., Diesmann, M.: NEST (NEural Simulation Tool). Scholarpedia **2**(4), 1430 (2007)
6. Lebenberg, J., et al.: A framework based on sulcal constraints to align preterm, infant and adult human brain images acquired in vivo and post mortem. Brain Struct. Funct. **223**(9), 4153–4168, December 2018

7. Lytton, W.W., Seidenstein, A.H., Dura-Bernal, S., McDougal, R.A., Schürmann, F., Hines, M.L.: Simulation neurotechnologies for advancing brain research: parallelizing large networks in NEURON. Neural Comput. **28**(10), 2063–2090 (2016). https://doi.org/10.1162/NECO_a_00876

8. Schmitt, S., et al.: Neuromorphic hardware in the loop: training a deep spiking network on the BrainScaleS wafer-scale system. In: 2017 International Joint Conference on Neural Networks (IJCNN), pp. 2227–2234 (2017). https://doi.org/10.1109/IJCNN.2017.7966125

Independent Component Analysis for Noise and Artifact Removal in Three-Dimensional Polarized Light Imaging

Kai Benning[1,2(✉)], Miriam Menzel[1], Jan André Reuter[1] ⓘ, and Markus Axer[1,2]

[1] Institute of Neuroscience and Medicine (INM-1), Forschungszentrum Jülich,
52425 Jülich, Germany
{k.benning,m.menzel,j.reuter,m.axer}@fz-juelich.de
[2] Department of Physics, Bergische Universität Wuppertal,
Gaußstraße 20, 42119 Wuppertal, Germany

Abstract. In recent years, Independent Component Analysis (ICA) has successfully been applied to remove noise and artifacts in images obtained from Three-dimensional Polarized Light Imaging (3D-PLI) at the mesoscale (i.e., 64 μm). Here, we present an automatic denoising procedure for gray matter regions that allows to apply the ICA also to microscopic images, with reasonable computational effort. Apart from an automatic segmentation of gray matter regions, we applied the denoising procedure to several 3D-PLI images from a rat and a vervet monkey brain section.

1 Introduction

Studying the structure and function of the brain requires dedicated imaging techniques, allowing to map the highly complex nerve fiber architecture both with high resolution and over long distances. The neuroimaging technique *Three-dimensional Polarized Light Imaging (3D-PLI)* [1,2] was designed to reconstruct the three-dimensional orientations of nerve fibers in whole brain sections with micrometer resolution.

To remove noise and artifacts in 3D-PLI images, *Independent Component Analysis (ICA)* has successfully been used [10–12]. However, the ICA has only been applied to mesoscopic images with a resolution of 64 μm pixel size and not to microscopic images with a resolution of 1.33 μm pixel size so far. In order to resolve single nerve fibers, e.g. in the cerebral cortex, such a microscopic resolution is required. Light scattering, thermal effects, inhomogeneity of optical elements, or simply dust on the used filters are noise sources, which combined with the weak birefringence 3D-PLI signal in cortical areas inevitably lead to a low signal-to-noise ratio (SNR) and reconstruction errors.

Identifying and removing these noise components in microscopic 3D-PLI images is very challenging. The amount of data that has to be processed is extremely large and the sampling has to be done differently as compared to mesoscopic images. When applying the developed ICA method on microscopic

K. Amunts et al. (Eds.): BrainComp 2019, LNCS 12339, pp. 90–102, 2021.
https://doi.org/10.1007/978-3-030-82427-3_7

images, the characteristic differences of the signal strengths in white matter and gray matter brain regions need to be taken into account. As the birefringence 3D-PLI signal of densly packed nerve fibers (i.e., fiber bundles) of the white matter proceeding within the sectioning plane are very strong and show a higher SNR than the less dense fiber tracts present in the gray matter, the denoising procedure needs only to be applied in regions of gray matter, which massively reduces the required computing time.

Here, we present an automatic ICA denoising procedure for gray matter areas in microscopic 3D-PLI images. It consists of an automatic segmentation of gray matter, followed by a data-parallel ICA artifact removal with automatic classification of noise and signal activations.

2 Methods

2.1 Preparation of Brain Sections

Brain sections from a Wistar rat (3 months old, male) and a vervet monkey (2.4 years old, male) were selected for evaluation.[1] The brains were removed from the skull within 24 h after death, fixed in a buffered solution of 4 % formaldehyde for several weeks, cryo-protected with 2% DMSO and a solution of 20% glycerin, deeply frozen, and cut along the coronal plane into sections of 60 μm with a cryostat microtome (*Polycut CM 3500, Leica, Microsystems*, Germany). The resulting brain sections were mounted onto a glass slide each, embedded in a solution of 20% glycerin, cover-slipped, sealed with lacquer, and measured with 3D-PLI up to one day afterwards.

2.2 Three-Dimensional Polarized Light Imaging (3D-PLI)

3D-PLI reconstructs the nerve fiber architecture of the brain with micrometer resolution. By transmitting linearly polarized light through unstained histological brain sections and analyzing the transmitted light with a circular analyzer, the birefringence of the brain section is measured, thus providing information about the three-dimensional orientations of the highly birefringent nerve fibers (myelinated axons) in the tissue [1,2]. The 3D-PLI measurements were performed with the same setup as described in [23] (*LMP-1, Taorad GmbH*, Germany), using incoherent green light with a wavelength of about 550 nm. During the

---

[1] All animal procedures have been approved by the institutional animal welfare committee at Forschungszentrum Jülich GmbH, Germany, and are in accordance with European Union guidelines for the use and care of laboratory animals. The vervet monkey brain was obtained when the animal was sacrificed to reduce the size of the colony, where it was maintained in accordance with the guidelines of the Directive 2010/63/eu of the European Parliament and of the Council on the protection of animals used for scientific purposes or the Wake Forest Institutional Animal Care and Use Committee IACUC #A11-219. Euthanasia procedures conformed to the AVMA Guidelines for the Euthanasia of Animals.

measurement, the direction of polarization of the incoming light was rotated by $\rho = \{0°, 10°, \ldots, 170°\}$ and the transmitted light behind the circular analyzer was recorded by a CCD camera (*Qimaging Retiga 4000R*) for each rotation angle, yielding a series of $N = 18$ images. The pixel size in object space was about $1.33\,\mu m$. For each image pixel, the measured intensity values form a sinusoidal light intensity profile (*PLI-signal, $I(\rho)$*). The average value of the signal, i. e. the polarization-independent transmitted light intensity, is called *transmittance* and is a measure for tissue absorption and scattering (highly scattering tissue components such as nerve fibers appear dark in the transmittance image). The amplitude of the normalized signal is called *retardation* and indicates the strength of birefringence of the tissue. It is related to the out-of-plane angles of the nerve fibers in the brain section (in-plane nerve fibers show very high birefringence, while out-of-plane nerve fibers show much less [22]). The phase of the signal indicates the in-plane *direction* angle of the nerve fibers. Combining in-plane and out-of-plane angles, 3D-PLI allows to reconstruct the full three-dimensional orientations of the nerve fibers.

2.3   Segmentation of White and Gray Matter

Morphologically, brain tissue consists of two different tissue types: Gray matter and white matter. Gray matter contains various components, such as neuronal cell bodies, dendrites, synapses, glial cells, blood capillaries as well as myelinated and unmyelinated axons. Most of the gray matter regions are located at the outer surface of the brain (cortex), but also inner parts of the brain (i.e., sub-cortical nuclei) contain islands of gray matter. White matter is mainly composed of myelinated and unmyelinated axons. The largest portion of myelinated axons is located in the white matter.

For the ICA method presented here, it is necessary to consider gray matter regions separately from white matter regions.[2] In the following, we present a fully automated procedure to generate masks of white and gray matter.

As nerve fibers (myelinated axons) are highly birefringent, all regions with high birefringence signals (i. e. large retardation values $r > r_{\text{thres}}$ in the 3D-PLI measurement, cf. Fig. 1(a) in orange) can be considered as white matter. (The determination of threshold values such as r_{thres} will be described below.) On the other hand, regions with low birefringence signals ($r < r_{\text{thres}}$, Fig. 1(a) in blue) do not necessarily belong to gray matter, because regions with a small number of myelinated fibers, crossing nerve fibers, and nerve fibers that point out of the brain section (out-of-plane fibers) also yield low birefringence signals [22].

Studies by Menzel et al. [20] have shown that regions with crossing nerve fibers and regions with in-plane parallel nerve fibers yield similar transmittance values I_T, while regions with out-of-plane nerve fibers show lower transmittance values. Gray matter regions, on the other hand, show notably higher transmittance values. Hence, we can use the transmittance value in the region with

---

[2] Note that we here define white matter as all regions (/image pixels) that contain myelinated nerve fibers. Anatomically, some of these regions might be known as gray matter because they only contain a small amount of myelinated nerve fibers.

maximum retardation I_{rmax} as a reference value (we expect that this region contains mostly in-plane parallel nerve fibers) and can then define all regions with similar or lower transmittance values as white matter ($0 < I_{\mathrm{T}} \lesssim I_{\mathrm{rmax}}$, containing crossing and out-of-plane fibers). All other brain regions are considered to be gray matter. To separate brain tissue from background, we make use of the fact that the transmittance in the recorded images is expected to be much higher outside of the tissue than within the tissue ($I_{\mathrm{T}} > I_{\mathrm{lower}}$, cf. Fig. 1(b) in gray).

To enable an automated segmentation into white and gray matter regions, we consider the retardation and transmittance histograms (consisting of 128 bins, see Fig. 1 on top). Before computing the transmittance histogram, the values are normalized to $[0, 1]$ and a median filter with circular kernel (radius of 10 pixels) is applied to the image to reduce noise. While the retardation histogram shows usually only a single peak at very low retardation values (caused by background and gray matter), the transmittance histogram shows one peak for low transmittance values (white matter), another peak for larger transmittance values (gray matter), and a third peak for high transmittance values (background).

To compute the threshold value r_{thres} (I_{upper}), we determine the point of maximum curvature behind (before) the biggest peak in the retardation (transmittance) histogram, i. e. the position for which the angle difference between two neighboring data points becomes minimal. To ensure that the point of maximum curvature belongs to the onset of the biggest peak (and not to some other peak or outlier), we take the full width at half maximum (FWHM) of the peak into account and only search within $10\times$ FWHM behind the retardation peak and $2.5\times$ FWHM before the transmittance peak, taking the different forms of the histograms into account.

To compute I_{rmax}, the region with the maximum retardation value is determined. To ensure that the region belongs to a white matter region and is not an outlier caused by noise, we use the Connected Components algorithm from the OpenCV library [4] (block-based binary algorithm using binary decision trees [6]) with eightfold connectivity. We mark all pixels with maximum retardation value and count the number of pixels in the largest connected region. If the number is at least 512, we select this region as reference. If the number is lower, we reduce the maximum retardation value iteratively by 0.01, until we find such a region. In this reference region, we compute the average value in the normalized transmittance image (I_{rmax}, see red vertical line in Fig. 1(b)). This value can be used as first estimate to separate white from gray matter. To define the border more precisely, we use the point of maximum curvature between I_{rmax} and I_{upper} as new threshold value I_{lower}.

Taking all this into account, we can compute the masks for white and gray matter as follows:

$$\text{White Matter:} \quad (0 < I_{\mathrm{T}} < I_{\mathrm{lower}}) \vee (r > r_{\mathrm{thres}}), \tag{1}$$

$$\text{Gray Matter:} \quad (I_{\mathrm{lower}} \leq I_{\mathrm{T}} \leq I_{\mathrm{upper}}) \wedge (r \leq r_{\mathrm{thres}}). \tag{2}$$

All image pixels that fulfill Eq. 1 (Eq. 2) are considered as white (gray) matter, see Fig. 1(b) in white. All other image pixels are considered as background.

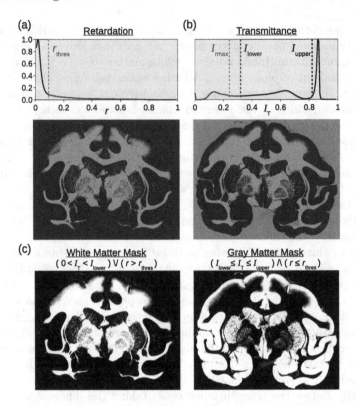

Fig. 1. Mask generation for white and gray matter, shown exemplary for a coronal vervet monkey brain section. **(a,b)** Top: Histograms of retardation and transmittance images obtained from a 3D-PLI measurement (128 bins in [0,1]); the determined threshold values are marked by vertical dashed lines. Bottom: Image pixels with values belonging to the orange, blue, and gray shaded regions in the histograms are marked in the respective colors. **(c)** Masks for white and gray matter, computed using the threshold values defined in the histograms on top. (Color figure online)

2.4   Independent Component Analysis (ICA)

The ICA belongs to the group of *Blind Source Separation (BSS)* techniques and can be used for data decomposition to find statistically independent components in a mixture of signals [17]. ICA has been applied to various artifact removal tasks, e.g. ocular artifact removal in electroencephalography [13], cardiac artifact removal in magnetoencephalography [5], and noise-signal-discrimination in functional magnetic resonance imaging [21].

In 3D-PLI, a data set consists of a series of N images (one for each rotation angle). To avoid that the background interferes with the decomposition, each image is divided into background and our region of interest (ROI) with the latter containing M pixels. The measurements are flattened and centered to obtain a zero-mean data array X with the dimension $N \times M$. The decomposition into sources S with the shape $N \times M$ requires that the data can be represented as a linear mixture of independent signals without additional additive noise, that there exist sufficient samples for every extracted feature (general advise is to keep $k \cdot N^2 \geq M$ with $k \in \{1, 2, 3, \dots\}$), and that the distribution of the sources is non-Gaussian. With these prerequisites, the problem can be stated as

$$X = AS, \tag{3}$$

where A is the so-called mixing matrix with the dimension $N \times N$ and is yet unknown. Because S and A are both unknown, it is impossible to make a prediction about sign or amplitude of the basis vectors of A. Furthermore, we have no knowledge about the number of components in our data set, so we assume that the complexity of the data can be mapped by N features.

Prior to performing the ICA, the data array X is whitened by making use of a *Principle Component Analysis (PCA)* [24] to lower the degrees of freedom to $N(N-1)/2$ [17]. The ICA then estimates $W \approx A^{-1}$ by maximizing the entropy as in Infomax-based ICA [3] or by maximizing a measure of non-Gaussianity as in FastICA [15,16]. We then obtain

$$WX = C \approx S, \tag{4}$$

with the component vector C. We find the activation profiles of the Components in W^{-1} as basis vectors. It was shown that 3D-PLI signals contain sub- as well as super-Gaussian independent components, therefore FastICA or Extended Infomax [19], an extension of the Infomax algorithm, can be used. This work uses the Extended-Infomax Implementation of the MNE-Toolbox [14].

2.5   Automatic Noise Removal with ICA

The activation profiles given by the ICA can be distinguished into two categories: noise activation profile and signal activation profile. Because we know the PLI-signal shape from theory, we know the shape of the basis vectors we are looking for in our mixing matrix $W^{-1} \approx A$. A simple classification problem is visualized in Fig. 2. The sinusoidal shaped activations are the ones to keep and we want to drop the activations that resemble random distributions.

The automatic identification is realized by fitting the expected (theoretical) function to each of the N activations. As identification measure, the mean squared error (MSE) is calculated for every fit and compared to the mean of all MSE values. When the MSE of the i-th fit is smaller than $1/10$ of the mean of all MSE values, we assume that the activation belongs to a signal component. Otherwise, we assume that the activation belongs to a noise component.

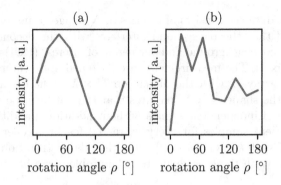

Fig. 2. Archetypal signal discrimination for ICA artifact removal: **(a)** sinusoidal PLI-signal activation, **(b)** random PLI-noise activation from e.g. thermal noise or light scattering.

After the detection of all noise activations, we construct a denoised mixing matrix $W_d^{-1} \approx A_d$ by just zeroing out the respective column:

$$
W_d^{-1} = \begin{pmatrix} - \text{ Signal Activation 1} - \\ - \text{ Signal Activation 2} - \\ \dots \\ - \text{ Signal Activation } J - \\ - \text{ Noise Activation 1} - \\ - \text{ Noise Activation 2} - \\ \dots \\ - \text{ Noise Activation } K - \end{pmatrix}^T = \begin{pmatrix} - \text{ Signal Activation 1} - \\ - \text{ Signal Activation 2} - \\ \dots \\ - \text{ Signal Activation } J - \\ - \qquad 0 \qquad - \\ - \qquad 0 \qquad - \\ \dots \\ - \qquad 0 \qquad - \end{pmatrix}^T .
$$

$$(5)$$

The denoised data array X_d can then be obtained by remixing the previously unmixed components:

$$
W_d^{-1} C = W_d^{-1} W X = X_d. \tag{6}
$$

Estimation of Signal Enhancement. The noise reduction of the artifact removal is measured with a weighted chi-square statistic introduced by [10]. It is based on the reduced chi-squared statistic defined by

$$
\chi^2 = \frac{1}{\nu} \sum_{i=1}^{N} \frac{(I(\rho_i) - f(\rho_i))^2}{\sigma(x,y,\rho)^2}, \tag{7}
$$

with ν for the degrees of freedom, N the number samples (here measurement angles), $I(\rho_i)$ the measured light intensity for an angle, $f(\rho_i)$ the expected function, and $\sigma(x,y,\rho)$ the standard error for every image point and angle. This statistic is applied to both noisy and denoised data leading to χ^2_{raw} and χ^2_{ICA}. We denote the quotient of these two measures by *relative Goodness of Fit (rGoF)*.

In case one component is missing and the denoised signal is inherently different, an additional weighting factor ω defined by

$$\omega = \frac{1}{\nu} \sum_{i=1}^{N} \frac{(f(\rho_i) - f^*(\rho_i))^2}{\sigma(x, y, \rho)^2} \tag{8}$$

is included in the denominator, which penalizes large deviations between the expected function of the noisy signal $f(\rho_i)$ and the expected function of the denoised signal $f^*(\rho_i)$. The so obtained measure is denoted by *weighted relative Goodness of Fit (wrGoF)*:

$$\text{wrGoF} = \frac{\text{rGoF}}{\omega} = \frac{\chi_{\text{raw}}^2}{\chi_{\text{ICA}}^2 \cdot \omega}, \tag{9}$$

where wrGoF > 1 is associated with a signal improvement while wrGoF < 1 is associated with a signal degradation.

Parallelization Concept. The parallelization is implemented by distributing the workload of the ICA problem equally in N parts to N workers via the Message Passing Interface (MPI) with mpi4py [7–9]. Every n-th element is sent to the n-th worker. After converging the result of all workers is collected and fused to the end result.

3   Results

The denoising procedure was applied to 22 brain sections (14 coronal rat brain sections and 9 coronal vervet brain sections). Every section was masked with a gray matter mask (as described in Subsect. 2.3) to remove background and white matter areas. In all cases, three components of interest were found, each with a sinusoidal activation function. The signal activations were kept and the noise activations were automatically removed. The resulting components and activations are shown exemplary for rat brain section no. 100 in Fig. 3.

The amount of wrGoF values are in all sections greater than one ($>99.9\%$) and mostly greater than ten ($>99\%$). A spatial distribution of the values is shown in Fig. 4 for the rat brain section (right) and a vervet brain section (left). In Fig. 5, three selected intensity profiles are shown for the rat brain section. Each individual profile shows an improvement and the denoised profile describes the measurement in a smooth way and is not influenced by outliers.

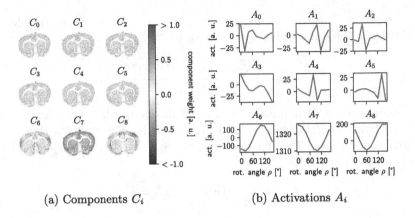

(a) Components C_i (b) Activations A_i

Fig. 3. Independent Components C_i for rat brain section no. 100 with their associated activations A_i. The noise components are in the first and second row, the signal components are in the last row.

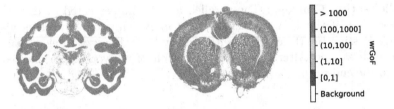

Fig. 4. Signal enhancement in a brain section visualized via the wrGoF measure. **Left**: wrGoF-map of vervet brain section no. 627. **Right**: wrGoF-map of rat brain section no. 100.

The alternating parallelization approach achieves a linear speedup of up to 12 cores (i. e. half of the cores on a node on the JURECA supercomputer [18]). The usage of all cores on the node only improves the speedup by two additional units as seen in Fig. 6. Overall, a weak scaling can be observed. While four nodes give a speedup of factor 2 with respect to one node, six nodes only offer a speedup of 2.5. For a complete vervet brain section (sample size $\sim 10^8$ pixels), the run time of the denoising routine for a single worker is about five hours. Using a whole node lowers this to half an hour, and using four nodes lowers the run time to 15 min.

This scaling behavior is the same for the rat and the vervet brain sections. Furthermore, the number of workers and therefore the number of partial ICA problems do not interfere with the quality of the denoising process. The percentage of wrGoF values greater than one ($>99.9\%$) or greater than ten ($>99\%$) are not influenced by the amount of parallelism.

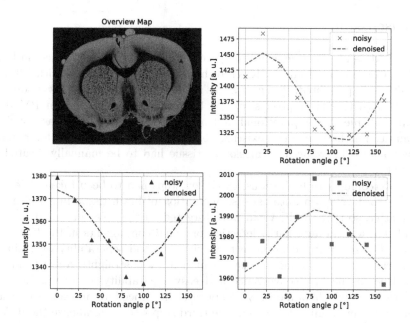

Fig. 5. Signal enhancement by the ICA denoising procedure shown for rat brain section no. 100: The image on the upper left shows the transmittance of the brain section for gray matter (background and white matter are displayed in black). The graphs show the intensity profiles of three selected areas (colored dots in transmittance image) before and after the denoising procedure.

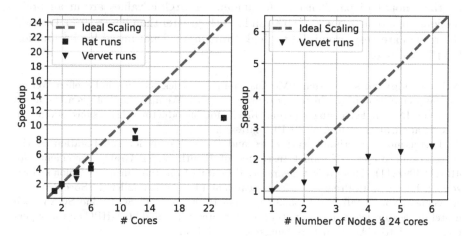

Fig. 6. Scaling behavior of the ICA denoising procedure. **Left:** Intra-node scaling behavior for 1–24 Cores. **Right:** Global scaling behavior.

4 Discussion

In this work, an automatic denoising procedure for 3D-PLI data based on Independent Component Analysis (ICA) for high-resolution PM data (with $1.33\,\mu m$ pixel size) was presented. Previous works studied the denoising of low-resolution LAP data (with $64\,\mu m$ pixel size) [10–12], but the application on PM data was limited due to computational and memory constraints and was not fully automatic. Furthermore, the existing solutions were not suitable for a high-throughput workflow because masks for tissue had to be manually created or adjusted.

To overcome these limitations, three key steps had to been taken: The first step was to develop an automatic segmentation of brain tissue into white and gray matter, so that the ICA can work targeted on the noisy gray matter. The second step was an automatic detection of signal components in the ICA activations. The investigated brain sections showed good separability by a simple MSE measure. The zeroing of noisy components was straightforward to implement. Due to the fast convergence and easy separability, there was no need for constraints which would only complicate the procedure and add expensive hyperparameter training as in [10]. The third step was to parallelize the ICA in a pleasingly parallel manner to evenly distribute the workload and ensure that each worker receive similar statistics. This showed a weak, but significant scaling as shown in Fig. 6.

The obtained results for the wrGoF measure were consistently better than the ICA denoising for LAP data presented in [10, 11]. The values were not influenced by the amount of parallelism. The amount of wrGoF values are in all brain sections greater than one ($>99.9\%$) and mostly greater than ten ($>99\%$). Overall, the results are very promising for high-throughput denoising of high-resolution 3D-PLI sections.

Acknowledgments. We thank Markus Cremer, Patrick Nysten, and Steffen Werner for the preparation of the histological brain sections. We also thank Jürgen Dammers from the INM-4, Forschungszentrum Jülich, for introductory discussions about the specific application of ICA to 3D-PLI datasets.

Furthermore, we thank Karl Zilles and Roger Woods for collaboration in the vervet brain project (National Institutes of Health under Grant Agreement No. 4R01MH092311). This project has received funding from the European Union's Horizon 2020 Framework Programme for Research and Innovation under the Specific Grant Agreement No. 785907 and 945539 ("Human Brain Project" SGA2 and SGA3). We gratefully acknowledge the computing time granted through JARA-HPC on the supercomputer JURECA [18] at Forschungszentrum Jülich.

References

1. Axer, M., et al.: A novel approach to the human connectome: ultra-high resolution mapping of fiber tracts in the brain. Neuroimage **54**(2), 1091–1101 (2011). https:// doi.org/10.1016/j.neuroimage.2010.08.075

2. Axer, M., et al.: High-resolution fiber tract reconstruction in the human brain by means of three-dimensional polarized light imaging. Front. Neuroinform. 5(34), 1–13 (2011). https://doi.org/10.3389/fninf.2011.00034
3. Bell, A., Sejnowski, T.: An information-maximization approach to blind separation and blind deconvolution. Neural Comput. 7, 1129–59 (1995). https://doi.org/10.1162/neco.1995.7.6.1129
4. Bradski, G.: The OpenCV library. In: Dr. Dobb's Journal of Software Tools (2000)
5. Breuer, L., et al.: A constrained ICA approach for real-time cardiac artifact rejection in magnetoencephalography. IEEE Trans. Biomed. Eng. 61(2), 405–414 (2014)
6. Chang, W.-Y., Chiu, C.-C., Yang, J.-H.: Block-based connected-component labeling algorithm using binary decision trees. Sensors 15(9), 23763–23787 (2015)
7. Dalcin, L.D., Paz, R.R., Storti, M.: MPI for Python. J. Parallel Distrib. Comput. 65(9), 1108–1115 (2005). https://doi.org/10.1016/j.jpdc.2005.03.010, ISSN 0743-7315
8. Dalcin, L.D., et al.: MPI for Python: performance improvements and MPI-2 extensions. J. Parallel Distrib. Comput. 68(5), 655–662 (2008). https://doi.org/10.1016/j.jpdc.2007.09.005, ISSN 0743-7315
9. Dalcin, L.D., et al.: Parallel distributed computing using Python. Adv. Water Resour. 34(9), 1124–1139 (2011). https://doi.org/10.1016/j.advwatres.2011.04.013, ISSN 0309-1708. New Computational Methods and Software Tools
10. Dammers, J., et al.: Automatic identification of gray and white matter components in polarized light imaging. Neuroimage 59, 1338–47 (2011). https://doi.org/10.1016/j.neuroimage.2011.08.030
11. Dammers, J., et al.: Optimized signal separation for 3D-polarized light imaging, pp. 355–374 (2013). https://doi.org/10.5772/55246, ISBN 9789535111603
12. Dammers, J., et al.: Signal enhancement in polarized light imaging by means of independent component analysis. Neuroimage 49, 1241–8 (2009). https://doi.org/10.1016/j.neuroimage.2009.08.059
13. Dimigen, O.: Optimizing the ICA-based removal of ocular EEG artifacts from free viewing experiments. NeuroImage, 116117 (2020). https://doi.org/10.1016/j.neuroimage.2019.116117
14. Gramfort, A., et al.: MEG and EEG data analysis with MNE-Python. Front. Neurosci. 7, 267 (2013). https://doi.org/10.3389/fnins.2013.00267, ISSN 1662-453X
15. Hyvärinen, A., Oja, E.: Independent component analysis: algorithms and applications. Neural Netw. 13(4–5), 411–430 (2000). https://doi.org/10.1016/S0893-6080(00)00026-5. Neural networks : the official journal of the International Neural Network Society
16. Hyvärinen, A.: Fast and robust fixed-point algorithms for independent component analysis. IEEE Trans. Neural Netw. 10(3), 626–634 (1999)
17. Hyvärinen, A., Karhunen, J., Oja, E.: Independent Component Analysis. Adaptive and Cognitive Dynamic Systems: Signal Processing, Learning, Communications and Control. Wiley (2004). ISBN 9780471464198
18. Krause, D., Thörnig, P.: JURECA: general-purpose supercomputer at Jülich supercomputing centre. Large-Scale Res. Facil. 4, A132 (2016)
19. Lee, T.-W., Girolami, M., Sejnowski, T.: Independent component analysis using an extended infomax algorithm for mixed sub-Gaussian and Super-Gaussian sources. Neural Comput. 11, 417–441 (1999). https://doi.org/10.1162/089976699300016719
20. Menzel, M., et al.: Toward a high-resolution reconstruction of 3D nerve fiber architectures and crossings in the brain using light scattering measurements and finite-difference time-domain simulations. Phys. Rev. X 2, 021002. https://doi.org/10.1103/PhysRevX.10.021002

21. McKeown, M.: Independent component analysis of functional MRI: what is signal and what is noise? Curr. Opin. Neurobiol. **13**, 620–629 (2003). https://doi.org/10.1016/j.conb.2003.09.012

22. Menzel, M., et al.: A Jones matrix formalism for simulating three-dimensional polarized light imaging of brain tissue. J. Roy. Soc. Interface **12**, 20150734 (2015). https://doi.org/10.1098/rsif.2015.0734

23. Menzel, M., et al.: Scattered Light Imaging: Resolving the substructure of nerve fiber crossings in whole brain sections with micrometer resolution. arXiv 2008.01037 (2020). https://arxiv.org/abs/2008.01037

24. Pearson, K.: On lines and planes of closest fit to points in space. Phil. Mag. **2**, 559–572 (1900). https://doi.org/10.1080/14786440109462720

Exascale Artificial and Natural Neural Architectures

Brain-Inspired Algorithms for Processing of Visual Data

Nicola Strisciuglio[1]([⊠]) and Nicolai Petkov[2]

[1] Faculty of Electrical Engineering, Mathematics and Computer Science,
University of Twente, Enschede, The Netherlands
n.strisciuglio@utwente.nl
[2] Bernoulli Institute, University of Groningen, Groningen, The Netherlands

Abstract. The study of the visual system of the brain has attracted the attention and interest of many neuro-scientists, that derived computational models of some types of neuron that compose it. These findings inspired researchers in image processing and computer vision to deploy such models to solve problems of visual data processing.

In this paper, we review approaches for image processing and computer vision, the design of which is based on neuro-scientific findings about the functions of some neurons in the visual cortex. Furthermore, we analyze the connection between the hierarchical organization of the visual system of the brain and the structure of Convolutional Networks (ConvNets). We pay particular attention to the mechanisms of inhibition of the responses of some neurons, which provide the visual system with improved stability to changing input stimuli, and discuss their implementation in image processing operators and in ConvNets.

Keywords: Brain-inspired computing · Image processing · Inhibition

1 Introduction

The development of the visual system of humans takes a number of phases, which include tuning the synaptic connections between neurons in the different areas devoted to the processing of different visual stimuli. In newborns, for instance, many connections between the Lateral Geniculate Nucleus (LGN), which is the first part of the brain devoted to visual processing, and the area V1 of the visual cortex are not formed yet. Similarly, the connections between neurons in the area V1 and subsequent areas start developing after the first month of life.

The tuning process of the receptive fields of the neurons of the visual system and the development of their inter-connected network can be compared to the training process of Artificial Neural Networks (ANNs). Since the beginning of their development, indeed, the design of ANNs has been largely inspired by the way the brain works, i.e. processing information via a network of neurons organized in a hierarchical fashion. Despite the resemblance of the Rosenblatt's perceptron with the physiological structure of a neuron, there is no actual relation between the processing of ANNs and the neural processes in the brain.

K. Amunts et al. (Eds.): BrainComp 2019, LNCS 12339, pp. 105–115, 2021.
https://doi.org/10.1007/978-3-030-82427-3_8

Many researchers in computer vision and image processing found inspirations from neuro-physiological studies of the visual system of the brain to design novel computational models that could process visual data. In 1959, Hubel and Wiesel carried out experiments on the visual cortex of cats and demonstrated the existence of the *simple cells*, which are neurons with an elongated receptive field. Their primary function is to detect edges and lines. Originally, the simple cells were modeled using Gabor functions [11,24] and used in image processing and computer vision applications, especially for texture description and analysis [16]. Subsequently, Hubel and Wiesel precised that simple cells receive inputs from certain co-linear configurations of the circular receptive field of neurons in the LGN [20]. Computational models based on Gabor functions were not able to describe all the properties of simple cells and ignored the contribution of LGN neurons for the processing of visual stimulti. In [4], a computational model based on the combination of the responses of Difference-of-Gaussians functions, which modeled the LGN receptive fields, was proposed. It achieved better contour detection performance than models based on Gabor functions and showed more properties of the simple cells in area V1 of the visual system of the brain, such as contrast invariant orientation tuning and cross orientation suppression.

Artificial neural networks (ANNs) and, in particular, convolutional neural networks (ConvNets) received much attention and showed some similarities with the visual system of the brain especially regarding its hierarchical organization. Although the training of neural network is formulated as an optimization problem and does not relate with biological processes, in [25] it was shown that the convolutional kernels learned in the first layer of AlexNet resembled the Gabor functions that were used to model the receptive field of neurons in the area V1 of the visual system. Similarly, unsupervised approaches for image analysis like Independet Component Analysis also learned features for image processing that resemble the Gabor-like receptive fields of neurons in area V1 [18].

Neuro-scientific and neuro-physiological studies of the mechanisms and systems that our brains uses to process external inputs have influenced also the developement of other branches of pattern recognition and artificial intelligence, such as sound signal processing. Patterson *et al.*, in 1986, modeled the response of the cochlea membrane in the inner auditory system as a bank of Gammatone filters [33]. They called Gammatonegram the result of the processing of an input signal by a Gammatone filter bank. Similarly to the spectogram, the Gammatonegram is a time-frequency representation of the sound in which the energy distribution over time and specific bandwidths is described. Parts of higher energy intensity correspond to regions of the cochlea membrane that vibrates more according to the energy of the mechanical sound pressure waves that hit the outer part of the auditory system. This model was exploited in [45–47] as input to a trainable feature extractor, the design of which was inspired by the activation of the inner hair cells, placed behind the cochlea, which convert the vibration into electrical stimuli on the auditory nerve.

This paper focuses on the relation between neuro-scientific studies and progress in Computer Vision and Image Processing, providing an overview of methods and aspects that concern detection and processing of low-level features in images until more complex computations in convolutional networks.

2   Brain-Inspired Processing of Visual Data

One of the pioneering architectures for image processing and computer vision inspired by knowledge of the brain processes of vision was the neocognitron network [13]. It modeled the hierarchical arrangement of the visual system of the brain by layers of S- and C-cell components, which are computational models of the simple and complex cells discovered by Hubel and Wiesel [20]. The weights of the neocognitron network were learned via an unsupervised training process, based on self-organizing maps. This training resulted in a hierarchy of S- and C-cell units that resembled the organization of the human visual system.

In the following of the section, some of these approaches are discussed, and part of the focus is given to the phenomena of inhibition that contribute to increase the selectivity of neurons to specific visual stimuli and how they are embedded in operators for processing of visual data.

2.1   Edge and Line Detection

Simple cells in area V1 of the visual cortex receive inputs from LGN cells in the thalamus of the brain and have the function of detecting elongated structures that contain high contrast information. The receptive fields of LGN cells are modeled by on- and off-center Difference-of-Gaussians (DoG) functions, while those of simple cells are modeled as co-linear arrangement of DoG functions. Originally, simple cells were modeled with Gabor functions, bypassing the contribution of the LGN cells. Computational models based on Gabor filters were used for contour and line detection and included in hierarchical architectures for object detection [36] and face recognition [34] tasks.

Although Gabor filters were used, initially, to model the simple cell receptive fields [24], they did not reproduce certain properties, such as contrast invariant orientation tuning and cross orientation suppression. These properties were achieved by a non-linear model, named CORF (Combination of Receptive Fields) for contour detection [4]. It is based on the combination of co-linearly aligned DoG functions, modeling the way simple cells combine the response of LGN cells. A mechanism for tolerance to curvature of lines and contours, based on a non-linear blurring, was proposed in the CORF model to improve the results when deployed in image processing pipelines.

An implementation of CORF, named (B-)COSFIRE (Combination of Shifted Filter Responses), where B- stands for bar-selective, was demonstrated to be successful for the detection of thick lines in images and applied to blood vessel delineation in retinal images (see Fig. 1) [7,41], road and river segmentation in aerial images [44], crack detection in pavement images [38]. An example of the response map computed by a B-COSFIRE filter and its thresholded binary map are shown in Fig. 1b and Fig. 1c, respectively. A curved receptive field was configured in [35], to detect high curvature points of the retinal vessel tree. In [40, 42], the authors demonstrated that a bank of B-COSFIRE filters, configured to delineate lines of different thickness, can be used as feature extractors and combined with a classifier to perform complex decisions.

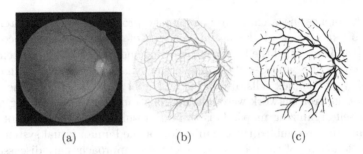

(a)   (b)   (c)

Fig. 1. (a) Example retinal image, the (b) response of the B-COSFIRE filter and (c) the corresponding binary map.

2.2 Object(-part) Detection

The response of neurons in area V1 are forwarded for further processing to neurons in areas V2 an V4 of the visual cortex, which are tuned to respond to sets of curved segments or vertices of some preferred orientation and badnwidth [32]. These properties can be interpreted as functions for detection of parts of objects.

Based on the principle of combining the responses of line and edge detectors at different orientations and with a certain spatial arrangement, an implementation of the COSFIRE model that takes as input a bank of Gabor filters of different orientation was released [3]. In this case, the receptive fields of neurons in area V1 that give input to those in area V4 were modeled by means of Gabor functions. However, a hierarchical structure of COSFIRE models can be realized for more complex tasks like object recognition or scene understanding [5]. The COSFIRE model of neurons in area V4 can be trained to detect parts of object and used in applications of object recognition. In Fig. 2, we show some examples of the parts of objects on which V4-COSFIRE models are trained. The light-blue ellipses indicate the location and the orientation at which the V1-like neuron responses are considered and their combination models a part of the object of interest. The configured models can be used to recognize parts of objects in other images or together in a filter-bank to extract feature vectors to be used in combination with a classifier.

2.3 Inhibition for Image Processing

One important aspect of the visual processes that happens in the visual system is the mechanism of inhibition. The receptive field of a simple cell, known as 'classical receptive field' [19], is composed of an excitatory and an inhibitory region.

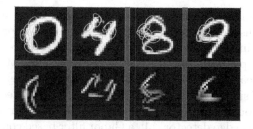

Fig. 2. The configured COSFIRE filters are represented by the set of light blue ellipses in the top row, whose orientation indicates the preferred orientation of the Gabor filter. In the bottom row, the part of the object that the corresponding COSFIRE filter is able to detect (figure from [3]). (Color figure online)

Many simple cells are know to receive push-pull (or antiphase) inhibition [21]. This form of inhibition happens when visual stimuli of given orientation and opposite polarity evoke responses of opposite sign [10,12,31]. Furthermore, it is known to be the most diffuse form of inhibition in the visual cortex [1]. In practice, for a stimulus of given polarity the response of the inhibitory receptive field suppresses the response of the excitatory receptive field.

This phenomenon was implemented in the CORF operator and it was demonstrated to be beneficial for improving contour detection in presence of texture [6]. More recently, the effect of the push-pull inhibition was shown to increase the robustness of line detection to various types of noise and textured background: a novel RUSTICO (Robust Inhibition-augmented curvilinear operator) operator was proposed in [37,39]. It was shown to be very effective for line detection in presence of noise and texture. RUSTICO is designed as an extension of the B-COSFIRE filter for line detection, by including an inhibitory component. In Fig. 3a and Fig. 3b, an aerial image of a river and the corresponding ground-truth are shown. The binary response map produced by RUSTICO (Fig. 3d) shows a more complete reconstruction of the line pattern of interest, i.e. the river, than that in the binary map produced by B-COSFIRE (Fig. 3c).

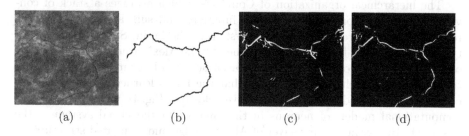

(a)   (b)   (c)   (d)

Fig. 3. (a) Aerial image of a river and (b) the ground truth of the river area. The (c) binary response map obtained by the B-COSFIRE filter is more noisy and contains less of the detected river patterns than the (d) binary response map of RUSTICO.

Another phenomenon of inhibition found in the visual cortex is the surround suppression. It consists of neurons, whose response is suppressed by that of neighbor neurons in the surrounding of their receptive field [9,49]. The cells that exhibit this type of inhibition have a non-classical receptive field (NCRF). Practically, this means that the response to a certain stimulus can be influenced by the presence of similar stimuli in the surrounding of the receptive field. This mechanism of surround suppression was included in image processing operators to extend the Canny edge detector [14], a Gabor filter based contour detector [15] and in an operator with a butterfly-shaped receptive field [50].

More recently, the push-pull inhibition and surround suppression were combined in a single operator for contour detection, which outperformed its counterpart operators with single or none inhibition mechanism [30].

3   Convolutional Networks for Visual Data Processing

Convolutional Neural Networks (ConvNets) became the *de facto* standard for image processing and computer vision, because of their effectiveness in dealing with various visual recognition tasks. Successful applications of ConvNets are image and object recognition [17], semantic segmentation [8], place recognition [2,27], image generation and image-to-image translation [22], among others.

ConvNets are based on convolution operations and exploit the characteristic of locality of the patterns of interest. This means that the value at a certain pixel location of a response map is detemined by the linear combination of the values of a small neighborhood of the corresponding pixel in the input image. From this perspective, ConvNets can be considered as a regularized version of multi-layer perceptron (MLP) networks. The fully-connectedness means that each neuron at a certain layer receives input from all the neurons in the previous layer. In a ConvNet, instead, each neuron (i.e. a convolution kernel) has a very limited number of inputs, and it slides over the input signal to compute its response. Although a single convolution catches local proprieties of the input signal in small-size neighboroods, the hierarchical organization of ConvNets allows to assemble more and more complex patterns in subsequent steps.

The hierarchical organization of ConvNets, which arranges a stack of convolutional layers, non-linear activation functions and sub-sampling operations resembles the hierarchy of the visual system of the brain. Speculations of this type were reinforced by the results obtained by the AlexNet network [25]. On top of the improvement of the classification accuracy by a large margin with respect to previous approaches, it was shown that the filters learned in the first layer of AlexNet resembled Gabor-like receptive fields (see Fig. 4), which are accepted computational models of neurons in the area V1 of the visual system of the brain [29]. Hence, in the first layer of AlexNet edge and elongated structures of different bandwidth are detected. The interpretations consist in that in subsequent layers, the detected edge and line patterns are combined into corner-like structures, similarly to the area V2 and V4 of the visual cortex, and into parts of objects (anterior and posterior TEO).

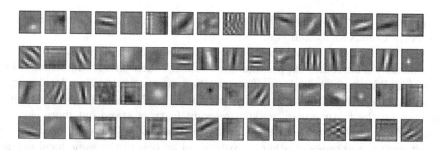

Fig. 4. Visualization of the convolutional kernels learned in the first layer of AlexNet.

The convolutions used in ConvNet architectures are linear operators and are not able to fully model some non-linear properties of the neurons in the visual cortex, e.g. response saturation or cross-orientation suppression. In [51], quadradic convolutions, in the form of Volterra kernels, were investigated and deployed as substitute of the convolution operations in existing architectures. This type of convolutions is more suited for a better approximation of the profile of the receptive fields of some neurons in the visual system. The approach was extended in [23], in which quadratic convolutional kernels contributed to reduce the depth, i.e. the total number of convolutional layers, of existing architectures while keeping the detection and classification performance of the corresponding deeper original networks.

On the one hand, the use of quadratic convolutions is justified by the closer connection with the function of the receptive field of the complex cells in the visual system, and contributed to a relatively small increase of performance. On the other hand, they require a much larger number of parameters to be learned, slowing down the training and increasing the complexity of the functions to be learned. In [51], indeed, due to computational limits, only the first layer of convolutions was replaced by Volterra kernels.

Another type of non-linear unit was proposed in [28], which incorporate the framework of the COSFIRE model of the neurons in the area V4 of the visual system into a new type of layer for ConvNets. The response of this layer is computed by combining the response maps of local simpler features according to a spatial structure that is determined in an automatic configuration step. During the training of the network, the CNN-COSFIRE layer can be configured to detect a certain arrangement of local features, so allowing for a larger receptive field that can catch non-local characteristics of the patterns of interest, such as parts of or entire objects. It was successfully demonstrated in applications of object detection and place recognition where few training samples are available.

3.1   Inhibition in Convolutional Networks

ConvNets learn representations, disentangling complex features of the training data. Inhibition is believed to be a mechanism for regularization and stability of the processes that happens in the visual system [26], and forms of inhibition are learned in ConvNets as well [48].

AlexNet deployed a layer called Local Response Normalizer (LRN), which implemented a surround suppression mechanism called lateral inhibition. This type of inhibition creates a form of competition among neurons in a local neighboround. The LRN builds on the idea of enhancing peak responses and penalizing flat ones on the feature map, making relevant features stand out more clearly. Thus, in the implementation, high local responses of one convolutional kernel inhibit weaker responses of other convolutional kernels in the same local neighbourhood. This serves as a form of regularization of the network and improves recognition performance.

In [43], a new type of layer that implements the push-pull inhibition mechanism was proposed, which can be used as a substitute of the convolutional layer. The push-pull layer can be trained with back-propagation of the gradient of the error and is interchangeable with any convolutional layer in the network. However, as it is inspired by neuroscientific evidence of inhibition mechanisms that occur in the early stages of the visual cortex, it was deployed as a substitute of the first convolutional layer only [43]. Using the push-pull layer in ConvNet architectures achieves better performance on image classification tasks when dealing with images that have been corrupted with noise or other types of artefacts (e.g. jpeg compression, blur, contrast changes and so on). Furthermore, when deploying the push-pull layer in ConvNets instead of a convolutional layer, the number of parameters to learn does not increase.

4   Conclusions

The research fields of image processing and computer vision were influenced by discoveries and progress in the understanding of the functions of neurons in the visual system. Computational models of different types of neurons formalized by neuro-physiological studies of their responses to visual stimuli have been deployed for image processing, especially related to low-level tasks such as line and contour detection.

In this paper, we reviewed the developments of edge and contour detection algorithms influenced by progress made in the understanding of the visual processes that occur in the visual cortex. We paid large attention to the importance that inhibitory mechanisms, namely push-pull inhibition and surround suppression, have on the robustness of the processing of visual stimuli in noisy and textured scenes. Furthermore, we covered the connections that neuro-physiological findings have with the development of Convolutional Networks and how inhibitory phenomena were explicitly implemented in the architecture of these networks with the aim of improving their stability to varying input stimuli.

Acknowledgments. Nicola Strisciuglio would like to thank Maria Rosaria Strisciuglio for the interesting discussions about the phases of learning and development of the visual system of the brain.

References

1. Anderson, J.S., Carandini, M., Ferster, D.: Orientation tuning of input conductance, excitation, and inhibition in cat primary visual cortex. J. Neurophysiol. **84**(2), 909–926 (2000)
2. Arandjelovic, R., Gronat, P., Torii, A., Pajdla, T., Sivic, J.: NetVLAD: CNN architecture for weakly supervised place recognition. In: IEEE CVPR, pp. 5297–5307 (2016)
3. Azzopardi, G., Petkov, N.: Trainable COSFIRE filters for keypoint detection and pattern recognition. IEEE Trans. Pattern Anal. Mach. Intell. **35**(2), 490–503 (2013). https://doi.org/10.1109/TPAMI.2012.106
4. Azzopardi, G., Petkov, N.: A corf computational model of a simple cell that relies on lgn input outperforms the gabor function model. Biol. Cybern. **106**, pp. 1–13 (2012). https://doi.org/10.1007/s00422-012-0486-6
5. Azzopardi, G., Petkov, N.: Ventral-stream-like shape representation: from pixel intensity values to trainable object-selective COSFIRE models. Front. Comput. Neurosci. **8**, 80 (2014). https://doi.org/10.3389/fncom.2014.00080
6. Azzopardi, G., Rodríguez-Sánchez, A., Piater, J., Petkov, N.: A push-pull CORF model of a simple cell with antiphase inhibition improves snr and contour detection. PloS one **9**(7) (2014)
7. Azzopardi, G., Strisciuglio, N., Vento, M., Petkov, N.: Trainable COSFIRE filters for vessel delineation with application to retinal images. Med. Image Anal. **19**(1), 46–57 (2015)
8. Badrinarayanan, V., Kendall, A., Cipolla, R.: SegNet: a deep convolutional encoder-decoder architecture for image segmentation. abs/1511.00561 (2015)
9. Bishop, P., Coombs, J.S., Henry, G.: Receptive fields of simple cells in the cat striate cortex. J. Physiol. **231**(1), 31 (1973)
10. Borg-Graham, L.J., Monier, C., Fregnac, Y.: Visual input evokes transient and strong shunting inhibition in visual cortical neurons. Nature **393**(6683), 369–373 (1998)
11. Daugman, J.G.: Uncertainty relation for resolution in space, spatial frequency, and orientation optimized by two-dimensional visual cortical filters. JOSA A **2**(7), 1160–1169 (1985)
12. Ferster, D.: Spatially opponent excitation and inhibition in simple cells of the cat visual cortex. J. Neurosci. **8**(4), 1172–1180 (1988)
13. Fukushima, K.: Neocognitron: a self-organizing neural network model for a mechanism of pattern recognition unaffected by shift in position. Biol. Cybern. **36**(4), 193–202 (1980). https://doi.org/10.1007/BF00344251
14. Grigorescu, C., Petkov, N., Westenberg, M.A.: Contour detection based on nonclassical receptive field inhibition. IEEE Trans. Image Process. **12**(7), 729–739 (2003)
15. Grigorescu, C., Petkov, N., Westenberg, M.A.: Contour and boundary detection improved by surround suppression of texture edges. Image Vis. Comput. **22**(8), 609–622 (2004)
16. Grigorescu, S.E., Petkov, N., Kruizinga, P.: Comparison of texture features based on Gabor filters. IEEE Trans. Image Process. **11**(10), 1160–1167 (2002)
17. He, K., Zhang, X., Ren, S., Sun, J.: Deep residual learning for image recognition. CoRR abs/1512.03385 (2015)
18. Hoyer, P.O., Hyvärinen, A.: Independent component analysis applied to feature extraction from colour and stereo images. Network Comput. Neural Syst. **11**(3), 191–210 (2000). https://doi.org/10.1088/0954-898X_11_3_302

19. Hubel, D.H., Wiesel, T.N.: Receptive fields of single neurones in the cat's striate cortex. J. Physiol. **148**(3), 574–591 (1959)
20. Hubel, D.H., Wiesel, T.N.: Receptive fields, binocular interaction and functional architecture in the cat's visual cortex. J. Physiol. **160**(1), 106–154 (1962)
21. Hubel, D.H., Wiesel, T.N.: Receptive fields and functional architecture in two nonstriate visual areas (18 and 19) of the cat. J. Neurophysiol. **28**(2), 229–289 (1965)
22. Isola, P., Zhu, J.Y., Zhou, T., Efros, A.A.: Image-to-image translation with conditional adversarial networks. In: CVPR (2017)
23. Jiang, Y., Yang, F., Zhu, H., Zhou, D., Zeng, X.: Nonlinear CNN: improving CNNs with quadratic convolutions. Neural Comput. Appl. **32**, 8507–8516 (2019)
24. Jones, J.P., Palmer, L.A.: An evaluation of the two-dimensional Gabor filter model of simple receptive fields in cat striate cortex. J. Neurophysiol. **58**(6), 1233–1258 (1987)
25. Krizhevsky, A., Sutskever, I., Hinton, G.E.: ImageNet classification with deep convolutional neural networks. In: NeurIPS, pp. 1097–1105 (2012)
26. Lauritzen, T.Z., Miller, K.D.: Different roles for simple-cell and complex-cell inhibition in V1. J. Neurosci. **23**(32), 10201–10213 (2003)
27. Leyva-Vallina, M., Strisciuglio, N., López Antequera, M., Tylecek, R., Blaich, M., Petkov, N.: TB-places: a data set for visual place recognition in garden environments. IEEE Access (2019)
28. López-Antequera, M., Leyva Vallina, M., Strisciuglio, N., Petkov, N.: Place and object recognition by CNN-based COSFIRE filters. IEEE Access **7**, 66157–66166 (2019)
29. Marĉelja, S.: Mathematical description of the responses of simple cortical cells*. J. Opt. Soc. Am. **70**(11), 1297–1300 (1980)
30. Melotti, D., Heimbach, K., Rodríguez-Sánchez, A., Strisciuglio, N., Azzopardi, G.: A robust contour detection operator with combined push-pull inhibition and surround suppression. Inf. Sci. **524**, 229–240 (2020)
31. Palmer, L.A., Davis, T.L.: Receptive-field structure in cat striate cortex. J. Neurophysiol. **46**(2), 260–276 (1981)
32. Pasupathy, A., Connor, C.: Population coding of shape in area v4. Nat. Neurosci. **5**(12), 1332–1338 (2002). https://doi.org/10.1038/nn972
33. Patterson, R.D., Moore, B.C.J.: Auditory filters and excitation patterns as representations of frequency resolution. In: Frequency Selectivity in Hearing, pp. 123–177 (1986)
34. Pinto, N., Stone, Z., Zickler, T., Cox, D.: Scaling up biologically-inspired computer vision: a case study in unconstrained face recognition on Facebook. In: CVPRW, pp. 35–42 (2011)
35. Ramachandran, S., Strisciuglio, N., Vinekar, A., John, R., Azzopardi, G.: U-COSFIRE filters for vessel tortuosity quantification with application to automated diagnosis of retinopathy of prematurity. Neural Comput. Appl. (2020). https://doi.org/10.1007/s00521-019-04697-6
36. Serre, T., Wolf, L., Poggio, T.: Object recognition with features inspired by visual cortex. In: IEEE Computer Society Conference on Computer Vision and Pattern Recognition, CVPR 2005, vol. 2, pp. 994–1000. IEEE (2005)
37. Strisciuglio, N., Azzopardi, G., Petkov, N.: Robust inhibition-augmented operator for delineation of curvilinear structures. IEEE Trans. Image Process., 1 (2019). https://doi.org/10.1109/TIP.2019.2922096
38. Strisciuglio, N., Azzopardi, G., Petkov, N.: Detection of curved lines with B-COSFIRE filters: a case study on crack delineation. In: CAIP, pp. 108–120 (2017)

39. Strisciuglio, N., Azzopardi, G., Petkov, N.: Brain-inspired robust delineation operator. In: Leal-Taixé, L., Roth, S. (eds.) ECCV 2018. LNCS, vol. 11131, pp. 555–565. Springer, Cham (2019). https://doi.org/10.1007/978-3-030-11015-4_41

40. Strisciuglio, N., Azzopardi, G., Vento, M., Petkov, N.: Multiscale blood vessel delineation using B-COSFIRE filters. CAIP **9257**, 300–312 (2015)

41. Strisciuglio, N., Azzopardi, G., Vento, M., Petkov, N.: Unsupervised delineation of the vessel tree in retinal fundus images. In: VIPIMAGE, pp. 149–155 (2015)

42. Strisciuglio, N., Azzopardi, G., Vento, M., Petkov, N.: Supervised vessel delineation in retinal fundus images with the automatic selection of B-COSFIRE filters. Mach. Vis. Appl., 1–13 (2016). https://doi.org/10.1007/s00138-016-0781-7

43. Strisciuglio, N., Lopez-Antequera, M., Petkov, N.: Enhanced robustness of convolutional networks with a push-pull inhibition layer. Neural Comput. Appl. (2020). https://doi.org/10.1007/s00521-020-04751-8

44. Strisciuglio, N., Petkov, N.: Delineation of line patterns in images using B-COSFIRE filters. In: IWOBI, pp. 1–6. IEEE (2017)

45. Strisciuglio, N., Petkov, N.: Trainable cope features for sound event detection. In: CIARP, pp. 599–609 (2019)

46. Strisciuglio, N., Vento, M., Petkov, N.: Bio-inspired filters for audio analysis. In: BrainComp 2015, Revised Selected Papers, pp. 101–115 (2016)

47. Strisciuglio, N., Vento, M., Petkov, N.: Learning representations of sound using trainable cope feature extractors. Pattern Recogn. **92**, 25–36 (2019). https://doi.org/10.1016/j.patcog.2019.03.016

48. Tjøstheim, T.A., Balkenius, C.: Cumulative inhibition in neural networks. Cogn. Process. **20**(1), 87–102 (2019)

49. Wiesel, T.N., Hubel, D.H.: Spatial and chromatic interactions in the lateral geniculate body of the rhesus monkey1. Notes **27**, 47 (1966)

50. Zeng, C., Li, Y., Yang, K., Li, C.: Contour detection based on a non-classical receptive field model with butterfly-shaped inhibition subregions. Neurocomputing **74**(10), 1527–1534 (2011)

51. Zoumpourlis, G., Doumanoglou, A., Vretos, N., Daras, P.: Non-linear convolution filters for CNN-based learning. In: ICCV, pp. 4771–4779 (2017)

An Hybrid Attention-Based System for the Prediction of Facial Attributes

Souad Khellat-Kihel[1], Zhenan Sun[2], and Massimo Tistarelli[3(✉)]

[1] Computer Vision Laboratory, University of Sassari,
Viale Italia 39, 07100 Sassari, Italy
[2] Center for Research on Intelligent Perception and Computing, National Laboratory
of Pattern Recognition, Institute of Automation, Chinese Academy of Sciences,
Room 1605, Intelligence Bulding, 95 Zhongguancun East Road,
Beijing 100190, P. R. China
[3] Computer Vision Laboratory, Department of Biomedical Sciences and Information
Technology, University of Sassari, Viale S. Pietro 43/b, 07100 Sassari, Italy
tista@uniss.it

Abstract. Recent research on face analysis has demonstrated the richness of information embedded in feature vectors extracted from a deep convolutional neural network. Even though deep learning achieved a very high performance on several challenging visual tasks, such as determining the identity, age, gender and race, it still lacks a well grounded theory which allows to properly understand the processes taking place inside the network layers. Therefore, most of the underlying processes are unknown and not easy to control. On the other hand, the human visual system follows a well understood process in analyzing a scene or an object, such as a face. The direction of the eye gaze is repeatedly directed, through purposively planned saccadic movements, towards salient regions to capture several details. In this paper we propose to capitalize on the knowledge of the saccadic human visual processes to design a system to predict facial attributes embedding a biologically-inspired network architecture, the HMAX. The architecture is tailored to predict attributes with different textural information and conveying different semantic meaning, such as attributes related and unrelated to the subject's identity. Salient points on the face are extracted from the outputs of the S2 layer of the HMAX architecture and fed to a local texture characterization module based on LBP (Local Binary Pattern). The resulting feature vector is used to perform a binary classification on a set of pre-defined visual attributes. The devised system allows to distill a very informative, yet robust, representation of the imaged faces, allowing to obtain high performance but with a much simpler architecture as compared to a deep convolutional neural network. Several experiments performed on publicly available, challenging, large datasets demonstrate the validity of the proposed approach.

1 Introduction

In the last decade, soft biometric traits have been widely used for person identification because of the robustness to noise, non-intrusiveness, and privacy preser-

K. Amunts et al. (Eds.): BrainComp 2019, LNCS 12339, pp. 116–127, 2021.
https://doi.org/10.1007/978-3-030-82427-3_9

vation. In the last years Deep learning approaches have been proposed also to extract soft-biometric attributes from face images. However, the high performance achieved are always paired with the requirement for high computational power and a large dataset for training. Liu et al. [1] proposed a method based on two CNNs which are trained for face localization (LNet) and attributes prediction (ANet). The top network layer, FC is exploited to learn identity-related features, such as the gender and race. Layers C3 and C4 are exploited to extract Identity-unrelated attributes, such as the facial expression, wearing hat and sunglasses. Samangouei et al. [2–4] proposed a CNN architecture suitable for mobile devices, which is based on the analysis of face parts. Recently, Dhar et al. [5] considered the usefulness of the outputs of the internal layers of two deep convolutional networks, Resnet 101 and Inception Resnet v2, for the prediction of facial attributes. Izadi [6] proposed the fusion of the extracted facial attributes with the face image to perform face recognition on a shared CNN architecture. Recently different works [7,8] proved that the final representation computed by a deep convolutional neural network embeds information not only about identity but also on the head pose and illumination. In this paper we propose to extract information from internal layer corresponding to HMAX network with the purpose of predicting different facial attributes. The HMAX model, which has been developed before deep learning took over in many computer vision problems, demonstrated the feasibility of a biologically-inspired neural architecture for face recognition. The model was tested on several publicly available databases such as LFW, PubFig and SURF-W [9] providing results at the state of the art. In [10], a new C3EF layer, inspired by the ventral and dorsal streams of the visual cortex, has been added to perform view-independent face recognition. Hu [11] proposed a version of the HMAX model, named 'sparse HMAX', addressing the local-to-global structure of the hierarchy, where the S2 bases are learned by sparse coding. In this paper we propose a novel hybrid system based on the HMAX network architecture. The outputs of the internal S2 layer are used as the seeds for extracting interest regions which are then used to generate the feature vector for the classification of the facial attributes. The following issues are addressed:

- How the salient feature points extracted from the HMAX architecture can improve the prediction of facial attributes.
- To which extent the devised system can be applied to predict different kinds of facial attributes.
- What is the robustness of an attentitive visual system to variations in head pose, lighting and facial expression.

2   Prediction of Facial Attributes

Most of the time celebrities or familiar people are remembered because of their special hair style, accessories or even clothes. This daily life concept is exploited by soft biometrics, or general visual attributes. These attributes can add significant information to face images and are quite robust to image degradation and changes in appearance. For this purpose, the internal S2 layer of the HMAX is used to detect the most salient points on the subject's face. The Linear Binary Pattern feature extractor is exploited to build a local description of the image texture around the selected points. The feature vectors computed for each salient point are concatenated to produce a global feature vector to characterize the face image. The obtained feature vector is fed to a SVM binary classifier to predict several visual attributes. In Fig. 1 the general architecture of the proposed framework is shown.

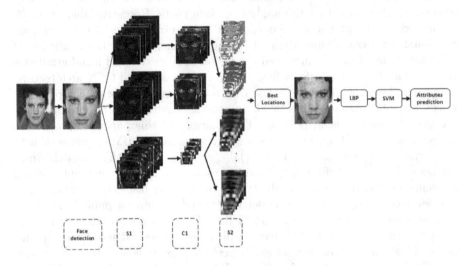

Fig. 1. Proposed hybrid system for the prediction of facial attributes.

2.1 The Hierarchical HMAX Network

HMAX is an hierarchical system that closely follows the organization of visual cortex and builds an increasingly complex and invariant feature representation by alternating between a template matching and max pooling [12]. As the network structure is fixed, a limited number of training examples is required for learning. The computational process is hierarchical and it is also invariant to position, scale and view-point. Along the hierarchy, the size of the receptive fields and the complexity of their optimal stimuli increases. The model consists of four computational layers, where *simple* 'S' units alternate with *complex* 'C' units.

The first layer S1 in the HMAX network consists of a bank of Gabor filters applied to the full resolution image. The response to a particular filter G, of layer S, at the pixel position (X,Y) is given by:

The first layer of the HMAX model 'S1' consists of a bank of Gabor filter, the following steps are implemented in (Fig. 2): The Image (at finest scale) is [256 * 256 * 1]. In each image intensity, four Gabor filters are applied over

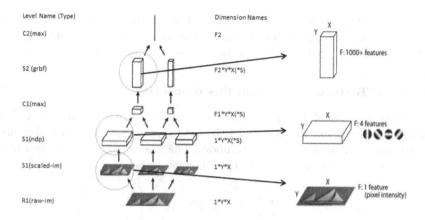

Fig. 2. General architecture of the HMAX model.

each pixel position. The result of S1 layer (at finest scale) is [246 * 246 * 4]. The response of a patch of pixels X to a particular S1 filter G is given by:

$$R(X,Y) = \left| \frac{\sum X_i G_i}{\sqrt{\sum X_i^2}} \right| \tag{1}$$

The size of the Gabor filter is 11×11 and it is formulated as:

$$G(x,y) = exp(\frac{-(x^2\gamma^2Y^2)}{2\sigma^2})cos(\frac{2\pi}{\lambda}X) \tag{2}$$

Where $X = x\cos\theta - y\sin\theta$ and $Y = x\sin\theta + y\cos\theta$. x and y vary between -5 and 5, and θ varies between 0 and π. The parameters ρ (aspect ratio), σ (effective width), and λ (wavelengh) are set to 0.3, 4.5 and 5.6, respectively. For the local invariance (C1) layer, a local maximum is computed for each orientation. They also perform a subsampling by a factor of 5 in both the X and Y directions [13]. In the intermediate feature layer (S2 level), the response for each C1 grid position is computed. Each feature is tuned to a preferred pattern as stimulus. Starting from an image of size 256×256 pixels, the final S2 layer is a vector of dimension $44 \times 44 \times 400$. The response is obtained using:

$$R(X,P) = exp(\frac{||X - P||^2}{\sigma^2}) \tag{3}$$

The last layer of the architecture is the Global Invariance layer (C2). The maximum response to each intermediate feature over all (X, Y) positions and all scales are calculated. The result is a characteristic vector that will be used for classification. For the implementation of the HMAX model we use the tool proposed in [13] As the final layer (C2) is the features vector that corresponds to maximums obtained from each S2 output, which are 400 characteristics. These maximum correspond to a certain locations (best coordinates) that are the maximal responses for each patch and image. These coordinates are accumulated and projected into the original faces images and used as interest points.

2.2 Local Texture Description Based on LBP

LBP is a type of visual descriptor used for classification in computer vision. The idea of the texture extraction using LBP is to give to each pixel a code which depends on the gray scale of its neighbors. The gray scale of the central pixel (i_c) is compared to its neighbors in the following formula:

$$LBP(x_c, y_c) = \sum_{n=0}^{P} s(i_n - i_c)2^n \quad X = \begin{cases} 0, & x < 0 \\ 1, & x >= 0 \end{cases} \tag{4}$$

The LBP code of the current pixel is produced by concatenating the 8 values to construct a binary code. The center of each window corresponds to the interest points obtained from HMAX.

2.3 Binary Classification with Support Vector Machines

The SVMs are groups of learning techniques that are designated to solve problems of discrimination, i.e. to decide to which class a pattern belongs, or of regression, i.e. to predict the numerical value of a variable. The success of this method is defined by solid mathematical bases. The main objective of the SVM is like the perceptron principle but it consists not only into finding an hyper plan that separates perfectly the classes but also to find the optimal one that can separate perfectly the classes by maximizing the margin. They project the data in space of characteristics by using non-linear functions. In this space it builds the optimal hyper plan which separates the transformed data. The principal idea is to build a linear separation surface in the space of the characteristics which corresponds to a non-linear surface in the space entry (Figure 3 presents this non-linear transformation).

The Support Vector Machines approach passes through two steps: The train that consists of searching an optimal hyper plan of separation by maximizing the margin, with the resolution of a quadratic program and determination of

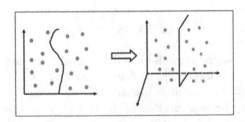

Fig. 3. The non linearity.

the Lagrange multipliers [14]. The test, after the determination of the Lagrange multipliers, it applies the decision function to the test examples to determinate the class [14]. The classification is conducted by using the SVM-KM toolbox [15] and by considering a Gamma value of 1e-7 and penalty parameter of the error term $C = 100$ while we use Gaussian kernel.

3   Experimental Results

Several publicly available large datasets have been used for testing the proposed architecture. The CelebFaces Attributes Dataset (CelebA) [1] is a large-scale face attributes dataset with more than 200K celebrity images each is notated with 40 attributes. The images in CelebA dataset include large variations in appearance such as pose and background. It contains 10.177 identities having 20 images in average. The CelebA does not overlap with LFW dataset identities. We also use the LFW dataset [16] which is a large dataset, real-world face dataset consisting of 13.000 images of faces collected from internet. These images are taken in completely uncontrolled situations. This dataset contains variations in pose, lighting, expression, camera, imaging conditions. CelebA and LFW were intensively used in the recent proposed work in the litterature for the aim to predict facial attributes. The PubFig dataset [19] has been used to test the sensitivity to variations in pose, illumination and facial expression. The PubFig dataset is a large, real-world face dataset (including both celebrities and politicians) consisting of 58797 images of 200 subjects collected from the internet. The PubFig dataset is both larger and deeper, on average 300 images per individual than previous seen dataset. These images are taken in completely uncontrolled situations. This database contains variations in pose, lighting, expression, camera, imaging conditions. The PubFig dataset is similar to LFW dataset. However, the PubFig dataset has enough examples per each subject.

Experiment 1: The first experiment consists of the facial attributes prediction using the Labeled Faces in the Wild (LFW) and the CelebFaces dataset. Table 1 and Table 2 represent the facial attributes prediction results using CelebA and LFW accordingly. In this experiment we propose also to compare our proposed system (internal layer) for attributes prediction with the top layers corresponding to HMAX, VGG, Alexnet and ResNet-50. Alexnet is a convolutional neural network that is trained on more than a million images from the ImageNet database [19]. The network is 8 layers deep and it can classify the images into 1000 object categories [20,21]. The network has an image input size of 227-by-227. ResNet-50 is also a CNN framework trained with the images from ImageNet [19]. It is 50 layers deep with an input size of 224-by-224. But unlike Alexnet, Resnet-50 layers are organised in residual blocks. With each block encompassing of at-least 3 CNN layers (1×1; 3×3; and 1×1 convolutions) followed by a shortcut connection. VGG is a convolutional neural network that is trained on more than a million images from the ImageNet database. The network is 16 layers deep and can classify images into 1000 object categories, such as keyboard, mouse, pencil, and many animals. As a result, the network has learned rich feature representations for a wide range of images [20]. This experiment is for the aim to compare between the proposed system that is based on internal layer and the final layers corresponding to the HMAX, VGG, Alexnet and Resnet-50.

Experiment 2: In the second experiment we propose to compare the obtained results on LFW and CelebA faces with some recent obtained results in the state of the art such as FaceTracer [17], PANDA [18], LNets+ANet [3] and Shared CNN proposed in [8]. Table 3 and Table 4 represent the results on LFW and CelebA datasets respectively. The aim of this experiment is to compare our proposed hybrid architecture with recently proposed systems in the litterature based on DNNs.

Experiment 3: In the third experiment, we test the PubFig dataset as it contains a large number of images per each subject. We study the efficiency of our proposed system on pose variation, faces under different illumination and expression. As the PubFig dataset contains images from the web a lot of them are not available, for this reason we construct a database composed of 54 subjects with 8942 images. Table 5 represents the obtained results which were compared also with Alexnet, VGG and Resnet-50 features.

From the obtained results (Table 1, Table 2), one can see clearly that the LFW dataset obtain better results with our hybrid system comparing to the CelebA and this is mainly due to the fact that we used CelebA faces in nonuniform order for the identities because the CelebA is composed of thousand of identities with twenty images per identity in average, these twenty images are dispatched randomly in the data; however, in the LFW database all the images corresponding to the same subject are in a successive order. Our proposed system demonstrate a comparable efficiency with the pretrained Deep Neural Networks (VGG, Alexnet and Resnet-50) in the same time surpass the obtained results with the features obtained from the final layer C2 corresponding to HMAX. Some facial attributes such as 'Attractive', 'Gray Hair', 'Male', 'Mustache' were well predicted using our model comparing to the pretrained DCNNs. In addition, our proposed biological system shows good performances comparing to the proposed models in the state of the art [3,8,17,18] specially on identity facial attributes. These identity-based facial attributes such as 'gender', 'hair color', 'nose' and 'lips shape', 'chubby' and 'Blad' can add meaningful information for face identification. Additionally, the proposed hybrid attention-based system achieve a comparable results with the final layers of VGG, AlexNet, ResNet-50 and HMAX. Another advantage is that our model use different locations to predict the whole attributes faces. However, LNets-ANets [1] use different layers to predict different kind of attributes, also [3] consider the fusion of different and specific regions from the face to detect a specific facial attribute. In the latest case we may not find all facial regions available specially with different poses on mobile devices. Even though the PubFig is very challenging database with variation in pose, illumination and expression, our proposed approach can distinguish between frontal and dark lighting images.

Table 1. Facial attributes prediction accuracies on LFW.

Attribute	HMAX	VGG	Alexnet	Resnet	Ours
5 o Clock Shadow	79.5	93	95.5	97.5	95
Arched Eyebrows	91	98.5	98.5	99.5	96
Attractive	76	95	96	93.5	96.5
Bags Under Eyes	86	92	95.5	96	91
Bald	95	99	98	98.5	95
Bangs	83	96.5	97	97.5	90
Big Lips	66	92.5	92.5	89.5	88
Big Nose	94.5	99.5	99	99.5	88
Black hair	99.5	99.5	99.5	99.5	86
Blond hair	100	100	99.5	100	93
Blurry	72.5	97	96	97	92
Brown hair	99.5	100	99.5	99.5	89
Bushy Eyebrows	84.5	95	96	96	86
Chubby	96.5	97.5	99.5	99.5	90
Double Chin	88.5	94.5	98.5	99	96
Eyeglasses	74.5	93	95	95	92
Goatee	84.5	97.5	97.5	97.5	91
Gray Hair	45.5	32.5	27.5	24	91
Heavy Makeup	99	100	98	99.5	91
High Cheekbones	72.5	96	96	95	88
Male	55	56.5	57	64	91
Mouth Slightly Open	45	46.5	46	34.5	91
Mustache	70	85.5	87.5	88	91
Narrow Eyes	81.5	83	91	88.5	88
No Beard	85.5	95.5	98.5	98.5	91
Oval face	88	98.5	97.5	97.5	91
Pale Skin	99	99.5	99.5	100	89
Pointy Nose	71	93	92	95	90
Receding Hairline	66.5	89.5	91	77.5	90
Rosy Cheeks	99	99	99	99	91
Sideburns	80	93.5	96.5	96	93
Smiling	88	96.5	96.5	97	94
Straight Hair	87	95.5	98.5	96.5	93
Wavy hair	75.5	88.5	94.5	94.5	89
Wearing Earings	86.5	96.5	96	97	92
Wearing Hat	68	91	93.5	89.5	88
Wearing Lipstick	91	99	98.5	97.5	90
Wearing Necklace	72	93	98	97	88
Wearing Necktie	99	98	99.5	99.5	93
Young	100	100	100	100	88

Table 2. Facial attributes prediction accuracies on CelebA.

Attribute	HMAX	VGG	Alexnet	Resnet	Ours
5 o Clock Shadow	85.4	88.2	88.2	88.2	91.5
Arched Eyebrows	96.8	77.2	77.6	76	60.5
Attractive	71.2	77.6	77.2	75.6	59.5
Bags Under Eyes	71.8	79.6	79.8	78.6	74
Bald	97.4	97.4	97.4	97.4	99.5
Bangs	81.8	87.2	87	88.8	82.5
Big Lips	64.6	75.2	75.4	74.6	60
Big Nose	70.4	78	77.4	77	74
Black hair	69.6	75.6	75.6	77.6	85
Blond hair	80.8	86.8	84.4	88	80.5
Blurry	93.8	94	93.6	93.6	99.5
Brown hair	71.4	78	78.4	77.4	81
Bushy Eyebrows	78	83.4	83.4	83	86
Chubby	92.6	95.8	95.4	95.4	96.5
Double Chin	94.4	95.6	95	95.4	97.5
Eyeglasses	91.4	97.8	97.6	96	97.5
Goatee	91.2	92.4	92	92.4	97.5
Gray Hair	93.6	94.2	93.8	94	98
Heavy Makeup	75.2	82.2	80.6	83.8	59.5
High Cheekbones	62.8	73	68.2	73.8	64.5
Male	73.6	79.6	81	84	83.5
Mouth Slightly Open	55.6	62	62.4	66.2	50
Mustache	94.8	95.6	95.6	95.2	96.5
Narrow Eyes	82.4	89.2	89	89.2	87
No Beard	81.4	84.4	83.4	84.6	91
Oval face	64.4	71.2	71.4	71	94.5
Pale Skin	95.6	96.8	96.2	96.6	98.5
Pointy Nose	66.6	72.6	72.2	71	67
Receding Hairline	91.2	94.8	95	94.6	95.5
Rosy Cheeks	92.4	94.2	94	94.2	85
Sideburns	92.6	93.6	93.2	93.6	96
Smiling	62.6	71	68.2	75.2	58
Straight Hair	73.6	81	81.2	81	84
Wavy hair	66.4	66.8	65.8	71.8	64.5
Wearing Earings	72.4	82	80.6	82.2	57
Wearing Hat	95	97	96.4	97.4	99
Wearing Lipstick	75	82.8	80.8	85.8	74
Wearing Necklace	79	86.4	85.6	86.2	77
Wearing Necktie	86.4	91.4	91.2	91.4	97.5
Young	73.6	80	79.6	76.8	81

Table 3. Comparaison of the attribute prediction frameworks on LFW

	Bald	Big Lips	Big Nose	Chubby	Male	Black Hair	Blond Hair
FaceTracer	77	68	73	67	84	76	88
PANDA	84	73	79	69	92	87	94
LNets-ANet	88	75	81	73	94	90	97
Shared CNN	90	65	75	62	94	80	88
Our model	91	88	86	96	91	93	92

Table 4. Comparaison of the attribute prediction frameworks on CelebAFaces

	Bald	Big Lips	Big Nose	Chubby	Male	Black Hair	Blond Hair
FaceTracer	89	64	74	86	91	70	80
PANDA	96	67	75	86	97	85	93
LNets-ANet	98	68	78	91	98	88	95
Shared CNN	97	67	79	91	99	75	84
Our model	99.5	60	74	96.5	83.5	85	80.5

Table 5. Comparison of the attribute prediction on PubFig database

	Pose	Lighting	Expression
HMAX features	60	61	50.3
VGG features	70.40	70.7	48.1
Alexnet features	70.8	69.7	49.7
Resnet features	71	69.9	51.5
Ours	70.9	70.9	51.4

4   Conclusion

In this paper a visual attention-based system have been proposed to predict the facial attributes. This hybrid system allows a biological hierarchical network 'HMAX' to look into a particular salient regions of the input faces in the same time reduce the complexity by discarding the irrelevant information. These regions were introduced to LBP with the aim of extracting texture feature around these interest points extracted with HMAX. This proposed framework shows a promising results comparing to Deep Neural Networks architectures. The success of the hybrid architecture is due not only to the biological vision perception but also to the possibility and flexibility of this approach to learn and treat small amount of data and predict different facial attributes. By surpassing these issues we can solve the main problem of DCNNs that require large amount of data for training. The proposed approach can add a good impact on face recognition as it can predict the most challenging real-world scenario (different background, pose variation, illumination, expression) that can degrade significantly the face recognition performances.

References

1. Liu, Z., Luo, P., Wang, X., Tang, X.: Deep learning face attributes in the wild. In: 2015 IEEE International Conference on Computer Vision (ICCV), Santiago, pp. 3730–3738 (2015). https://doi.org/10.1109/ICCV.2015.425
2. Samangouei, P., Chellappa, R.: Convolutional neural networks for attribute-based active authentication on mobile devices. In: 2016 IEEE 8th International Conference on Biometrics Theory, Applications and Systems (BTAS), Niagara Falls, NY, pp. 1–8 (2016)
3. Samangouei, P., Patel, V.M., Chellappa, R.: Attribute-based continuous user authentication on mobile devices. In: 2015 IEEE 7th International Conference on Biometrics Theory, Applications and Systems (BTAS), Arlington, VA, pp. 1–8 (2015)
4. Samangouei, P., Patel, V.M., Chellappa, R.: Facial attributes for active authentication on mobile devices. Image Vis. Comput. **58**, 181–192 (2017). ISSN 0262-8856
5. Dhar, P., Bansal, A., Castillo, C., Gleason, J., Phillips, P.J., Chellappa, R.: How are attributes expressed in face DCNNs?, arXiv preprint arXiv:1910.05657 (2019)
6. Izadi, M.R.: Feature Level Fusion from Facial Attributes for Face Recognition, arXiv preprint arXiv: 1909.13126, September 2019
7. Khellat-Kihel, S., Lagorio, A., Tistarelli, M.: Foveated vision for deepface recognition. In: Nyström, I., Hernández Heredia, Y., Milián Núñez, V. (eds.) CIARP 2019. LNCS, vol. 11896, pp. 31–41. Springer, Cham (2019). https://doi.org/10.1007/978-3-030-33904-3_3
8. O'Toole, A.J., Castillo, C.D., Padre, C.J., Hill, M.Q., Chellappa, R.: Face space representations in deep convolutional neural networks. Trends Cogn. Sci. **22**(9), 1364–6613 (2018)
9. Liao, Q., Leibo, J.Z., Poggio, T.: Learning invariant representations and applications to face verification. In: NIPS 2013 Proceedings of the 26th International Conference on Neural Information Processing Systems, Lake Tahoe, Nevada, vol. 2, pp. 3057–3065 (2013)
10. Esmaili, S., Maghooli, K., Motie Nasrabadi, A.: C3 effective features inspired from ventral and dorsal stream of visual cortex for view independent face recognition. Adv. Comput. Sci. 1–9 (2016). ISSN 2322-5157
11. Hu, X., Zhang, J., Li, J., Zhang, B.: Sparsity-regularized HMAX for visual recognition. PLoS ONE **9**(1), e81813 (2014). https://doi.org/10.1371/journal.pone.0081813
12. Riesenhuber, M., Poggio, T.: Hierarchical models of object recognition in cortex. Nat. Neurosci. **2**, 1019–1025 (1999). https://doi.org/10.1038/14819
13. HMAX toolbox. http://maxlab.neuro.georgetown.edu/hmax.html
14. Ayat, N.: Sélection automatique de modèle dans les machines à vecteurs de support: application à la reconnaissance d'images de chiffres manuscrits. Thèse de doctorat électronique, Montréal, École de technologie supérieure (2004)
15. Canu, S., Grandvalet, Y., Guigue, V., Rakotomamonjy, A.: SVM and Kernel Methods Matlab Toolbox. Perception Systemes et Information, INSA de Rouen, Rouen, France (2005)

16. Kumar, N., Berg, A.C., Belhumeur, P.N., Nayar, S.K.: Attribute and simile classifiers for face verification. In: 2009 IEEE 12th International Conference on Computer Vision, Kyoto, pp. 365–372 (2009). https://doi.org/10.1109/ICCV.2009.5459250
17. Kumar, N., Belhumeur, P., Nayar, S.: FaceTracer: a search engine for large collections of images with faces. In: Forsyth, D., Torr, P., Zisserman, A. (eds.) ECCV 2008. LNCS, vol. 5305, pp. 340–353. Springer, Heidelberg (2008). https://doi.org/10.1007/978-3-540-88693-8_25
18. Zhang, N., Paluri, M., Ranzato, M., Darrell, T., Bourdev, L.: PANDA: pose aligned networks for deep attribute modeling. In: 2014 IEEE Conference on Computer Vision and Pattern Recognition, Columbus, OH, pp. 1637–1644 (2014). https://doi.org/10.1109/CVPR.2014.212
19. http://www.cs.columbia.edu/CAVE/databases/pubfig/
20. ImageNet. http://www.image-net.org
21. Krizhevsky, A., Ilya, S., Geoffrey, E.H.: ImageNet classification with deep convolutional neural networks. In: NIPS 2012 Proceedings of the 25th International Conference on Neural Information Processing Systems, vol. 1, pp. 1097–1105 (2012)

The Statistical Physics of Learning Revisited: Typical Learning Curves in Model Scenarios

Michael Biehl[✉]

Bernoulli Institute for Mathematics, Computer Science and Artificial Intelligence,
University of Groningen, Nijenborgh 9, 9747 AG Groningen, The Netherlands
m.biehl@rug.nl
http://www.cs.rug.nl/~biehl

Abstract. The exchange of ideas between computer science and statistical physics has advanced the understanding of machine learning and inference significantly. This interdisciplinary approach is currently regaining momentum due to the revived interest in neural networks and deep learning. Methods borrowed from statistical mechanics complement other approaches to the theory of computational and statistical learning. In this brief review, we outline and illustrate some of the basic concepts. We exemplify the role of the statistical physics approach in terms of a particularly important contribution: the computation of typical learning curves in student teacher scenarios of supervised learning. Two, by now classical examples from the literature illustrate the approach: the learning of a linearly separable rule by a perceptron with continuous and with discrete weights, respectively. We address these prototypical problems in terms of the simplifying limit of stochastic training at high formal temperature and obtain the corresponding learning curves.

1 Introduction

At least two major developments have led to the regained popularity of machine learning in general and neural networks in particular [1–6]. Most importantly, the ever-increasing availability of training data from various domains and contexts have made possible the training of very powerful systems such as deep neural networks [4–6]. At the same time, the computational power necessary for the data driven adaptation and optimization of such systems, has become available.

Several concepts that had been developed earlier, some of them even decades ago, could be realized and applied successfully in practice only recently. Examples and further references can be found in [4–6]. In addition, novel computational techniques and important modifications of the considered systems have contributed to this success. This includes the use of pre-trained networks, sophisticated regularization techniques, weight sharing in convolutional neural networks, or the use of alternative activation functions [4–8].

While the relevance and success of the methods are widely recognized, several authors note that the theoretical understanding does not yet parallel the

© The Author(s) 2021
K. Amunts et al. (Eds.): BrainComp 2019, LNCS 12339, pp. 128–142, 2021.
https://doi.org/10.1007/978-3-030-82427-3_10

practical advances of the field, see for instance [9–13] in the context of deep learning. It is certainly desirable to strengthen and put forward the theoretical investigation of machine learning processes in general and deep learning in particular. The development of novel concepts and the design and optimization of practical training prescriptions would greatly benefit from better theoretical understanding. This concerns, for instance, mathematical and statistical foundations, the dynamics of training, and insights into the expected generalization ability of learning systems.

Concepts borrowed from statistical mechanics have been applied in many areas beyond the scope of traditional physics. In particular, analytical and computational approaches developed for the study of complex physical systems can be exploited within computer science and statistics. A prominent example is the use of Markov chain Monte Carlo methods [14], which exploit mathematical analogies between stochastic optimization and the statistical physics of systems with many degrees of freedom. Similarly, analytical methods which had been developed for the analysis of disordered systems [15], have been applied in this context.

A somewhat surprising and very inspiring analogy was pointed out by John Hopfield [16]: the conceptual similarity of simple dynamical neural networks with models of disordered magnetic materials [15]. It attracted considerable interest in neural networks and related systems within the physics community. Initially, the analysis of thermal equilibrium states in so-called attractor neural networks was in the center of interest [1, 16, 17]. However, the same concepts were applied successfully to the investigation of learning and synaptic plasticity in neural networks. Elizabeth Gardner's pioneering work [18, 19] paved the way for the theory of learning in a large variety of machine learning scenarios, including the supervised training of feedforward neural networks, methods of unsupervised data analysis, and more general inference problems, see [20–22] for reviews.

A variety of analytical tools and modelling frameworks have been developed and applied successfully to, for instance, the study of supervised learning in the context of regression and classification tasks. Mostly, relatively simple and shallow feedforward neural networks have been analysed [20–22]. Frequently, these training processes are modelled in the frame of a student and teacher scenario. There, a specific neural network, the teacher, is assumed to define the target task, e.g. a classification scheme. A student network is trained from a set of examples provided by the teacher and parameterizes a data driven hypothesis about the target rule. This allows to explicitly control the complexity of the target rule and of the learning system in the model. Moreover the performance of the trained system can be quantified in terms of its similarity and agreement with the teacher network. Learning can be interpreted as the stochastic optimization of many degrees of freedom, which motivates possible training algorithms based on statistical mechanics ideas. Also, analytical tools for the study of large systems in (formal) thermal equilibrium situations can be used, which describe the model in terms of a few macroscopic quantities, only. Frequently, these so-called order parameters appear naturally when analysing student teacher scenarios.

Ultimately, methods developed in the theory of disordered systems allow for the investigation of typical properties of the learning system. This concerns, for instance, the computation of learning curves as an outcome of the stochastic training process on average over the assumed randomness in the example data.

The successful applications of these concepts include, among other relevant topics, the highly interesting phenomenon of symmetry breaking phase transitions which result in discontinuous learning curves: Frequently, the success of training is found to depend critically on the number of available examples or other model parameters [20–25]. Currently, the interest in this type of analysis is gaining momentum again in the context of deep learning and other popular learning paradigms, see [26–31] for examples.

In the following section, we briefly outline and illustrate the statistical physics of student teacher scenarios in supervised learning. We present two variants of a simple and by now classical example: the learning of a linearly separable rule with a perceptron network with continuous or discrete weights, respectively. The perceptron has been discussed extensively in the literature and serves as a prototypical system for the understanding of machine learning processes, see e.g. [1, 20–22]. For the sake of brevity, we focus on a particularly simplifying approach, the consideration of stochastic training in the limit of high (formal) temperature. It was introduced and applied to perceptron training in [22]. Despite its conceptual simplicity and mathematical ease, this example illustrates the basic concepts very well and yields non-trivial results and insights into the learning process.

This contribution is based on a tutorial talk at the Workshop on Brain Inspired Computing, BrainComp 2019. It is obviously far from providing a complete overview of the statistical physics of learning. The intention is to attract the reader's attention in terms of selected example applications of the approach and to provide references as a starting point for further exploration of this highly relevant area of research.

2   Statistical Physics of Learning: Learning Curves

Typically, the statistical physics based computation of learning curves in supervised learning proceeds along the following steps:

1) A student and teacher scenario is defined, which parameterizes the target rule and fixes the complexity of the student hypothesis.
2) It is assumed that training examples and test instances are generated according to a specific input density, while target labels are provided by the teacher network.
3) The study of large systems in the thermodynamic limit allows to describe systems in terms of relatively few macroscopic quantities or order parameters.
4) The outcome of stochastic training processes is interpreted as a formal thermal equilibrium, in which thermal averages can be considered.

5) An additional disorder average over a randomly generated set of training data is performed in order to obtain typical results independent of the actual training set.

The following sections illustrate the above points in the context of learning a linearly separable rule [20–22], before two concrete example scenarios are analysed in Sect. 2.6.

2.1 Learning a Linearly Separable Rule: Student and Teacher

We consider the supervised learning of a linearly separable classification of N-dimensional data. In our model, the target rule is defined through a teacher perceptron with fixed weight vectors $\mathbf{w}^* \in \mathbb{R}^N$ and output

$$S^*(\boldsymbol{\xi}) = \text{sign}\left[\mathbf{w}^* \cdot \boldsymbol{\xi}\right] = \pm 1 \quad \text{for any } \boldsymbol{\xi} \in \mathbb{R}^N. \tag{1}$$

Here, the feature vector $\boldsymbol{\xi}$ represents N numerical inputs to the system and S^* corresponds to the correct output. The teacher weight vector parametrizes an $(N-1)$-dim. hyperplane which separates positive from negative responses.

We note that the norm $|\mathbf{w}^*|$ of the weights is irrelevant for the perceptron response (1). Throughout the following, we therefore consider normalized teacher weights with $\mathbf{w}^* \cdot \mathbf{w}^* = N$.

In the learning scenario, information about the rule is only available in the form of a data set which comprises P examples:

$$\mathbb{D} = \{\boldsymbol{\xi}^\mu, S^*(\boldsymbol{\xi}^\mu)\}_{\mu=1,2,...,P}. \tag{2}$$

Here we assume that the labels $S^{*\mu} = S^*(\boldsymbol{\xi}^\mu)$ provided in $\mathbb{D}$ are reliable and represent the rule (1) faithfully. We refrain from considering corruption by different forms of noise, for simplicity, and refer the reader to the literature for the corresponding extensions of the analysis [20, 21].

A second simple perceptron serves as the student network in our model. Its adaptive weights $\mathbf{w} \in \mathbf{R}^N$ parameterize a linearly separable function

$$S(\xi) = \text{sign}\left[\mathbf{w} \cdot \boldsymbol{\xi}\right]. \tag{3}$$

The weight vector $\mathbf{w}$ is chosen in a data-driven training process which is based on the available data $\mathbb{D}$ and corresponds to the student hypothesis about the unknown target. As a consequence of the invariance

$$\text{sign}\left[(\lambda\mathbf{w}) \cdot \boldsymbol{\xi}\right] = \text{sign}[\mathbf{w} \cdot \boldsymbol{\xi}] \quad \text{for arbitrary } \lambda > 0$$

we will also consider normalized student weights with $\mathbf{w} \cdot \mathbf{w} = N$ in the following.

2.2 The Density of Input Data

In realistic learning situations it is expected that the density of input features is correlated with the actual task to a certain extent. In real world classification problems, for instance, one would expect a more or less pronounced cluster structure which reflects the class memberships already. Clustered or more generally structured input densities have been considered in the statistical physics literature, see [26] for a recent discussion and further references. Here, however, we follow the most frequent approach and resort to the simplifying assumption of an isotropic input density which generates input vectors independently. In a sense, this constitutes a worst case in which the only information about the target rule is contained in the assigned training labels $S^*(\boldsymbol{\xi})$, while no gap or region of low density in feature space marks the class boundaries.

Specifically, we assume that components of example vectors $\boldsymbol{\xi}^\mu$ in $\mathbb{D}$ consist of independent, identically distributed (i.i.d.) random quantities with means and covariances

$$\langle \xi_j^\mu \rangle = 0, \quad \langle \xi_j^\mu \xi_k^\nu \rangle = \delta_{\mu\nu}\,\delta_{jk} \tag{4}$$

with the Kronecker symbol $\delta_{mn} = 1$ if $m \neq n$ and $\delta_{mm} = 0$.

2.3   Generalization Error and the Perceptron Order Parameter

The performance of a given weight vector $\mathbf{w}$ in the student teacher model can be evaluated with respect to a test input $\boldsymbol{\xi} \notin \mathbb{D}$. If we assume that the test input follows the same statistics as the training examples, i.e.

$$\langle \xi_j \rangle = 0, \quad \langle \xi_j \xi_k \rangle = \delta_{jk}, \tag{5}$$

we can define the so-called generalization error as the expectation value

$$\epsilon_g(\mathbf{w}, \mathbf{w}^*) = \langle \epsilon\left(S(\boldsymbol{\xi}, S^*(\boldsymbol{\xi}))\right)\rangle \quad \text{where} \quad \epsilon(S, S^*) = \begin{cases} 1 \text{ if } S \neq S^* \\ 0 \text{ else}, \end{cases} \tag{6}$$

serves as a binary error measure. Hence, the generalization error quantifies the probability for disagreement between student and teacher for a random input vector. It is instructive to work out ϵ_g explicitly under the assumption of i.i.d. inputs. To this end, we consider the arguments of the threshold function in student and teacher perceptron:

$$x = \mathbf{w} \cdot \boldsymbol{\xi}/\sqrt{N} \quad \text{and} \quad x^* = \mathbf{w}^* \cdot \boldsymbol{\xi}/\sqrt{N}.$$

Assuming that the random input vector $\boldsymbol{\xi}$ satisfies Eq. (5), x and x^* correspond to sums of N random quantities. By means of the Central Limit Theorem (CLT) there density is given by a two-dim. Gaussian, which is fully specified by first and second moments. These can be obtained immediately as

$$\langle x \rangle = \langle x^* \rangle = 0, \quad \langle x^2 \rangle = \frac{1}{N}\sum_{i,j} w_i w_j \langle \xi_i \xi_j \rangle = \frac{\mathbf{w}^2}{N} = 1, \quad \langle (x^*)^2 \rangle = \frac{(\mathbf{w}^*)^2}{N} = 1$$

$$\text{and} \quad \langle x\,x^* \rangle = \frac{1}{N}\sum_{i,j} w_i w_j^* \langle \xi_i \xi_j \rangle = \frac{\mathbf{w} \cdot \mathbf{w}^*}{N} \equiv R, \tag{7}$$

where we have exploited the normalization of weight vectors. The covariance $\langle x x^* \rangle$ is given by the scalar product of student and teacher weights. The moments

(7) fully specify the two-dimensional normal density $P(x, x^*)$ and we obtain the generalization error as the probability of observing $xx^* < 0$:

$$\epsilon_g(\mathbf{w}, \mathbf{w}^*) = \left[\int_{-\infty}^{0} \int_{0}^{\infty} + \int_{0}^{\infty} \int_{-\infty}^{0} \right] P(x, x^*) dx \, dx^* = \frac{1}{\pi} \arccos(R). \quad (8)$$

This result can be obtained immediately by an intuitive argument: The probability for a random vector $\boldsymbol{\xi}$ to fall into the hypersegments between the hyperplanes defined by $\mathbf{w}$ and $\mathbf{w}^*$ is directly given by $\angle\,(\mathbf{w}, \mathbf{w}^*)\,/\pi$ which corresponds to the right hand side of Eq. (8).

In the following, the overlap $R = \mathbf{w} \cdot \mathbf{w}^*/N$ plays the role of an order parameter. This macroscopic quantity summarizes essential properties of the N microscopic degrees of freedom, i.e. the adaptive student weights w_j. It is also the central quantity in the following analysis of the training outcome.

2.4 Training as a Stochastic Process and Thermal Equilibrium

The outcome of any practical training process will clearly depend on the actual choice of an algorithm and its parameters that is used to infer a suitable weight vector $\mathbf{w}$ from a given data set $\mathbb{D}$. Generically, the training process is guided by a cost function, such as the quadratic deviation of the student output from the target in regression systems or the number of incorrect responses in a classification problem.

Frequently, gradient based methods can be used for the optimization of continuous weights $\mathbf{w} \in \mathbb{R}^N$, often incorporating some form of noise as in the popular stochastic gradient descent. The search for optimal weights in a discrete space with, e.g., $\mathbf{w} \in \{-1, +1\}^N$ could be performed by means of a Metropolis Monte Carlo method, as an example.

The degree to which the system is forced to approach the actual minimum of the cost function is controlled implicitly or explicitly in the training algorithm. Example control parameters are the learning rate in gradient descent or the temperature parameter in Metropolis like schemes. In the statistical physics approach to learning, this concept is taken into account by considering a formal thermal equilibrium situation as outlined below.

In the context of the perceptron student teacher scenario we consider a cost function of the form

$$H(\mathbf{w}) = \sum_{\mu=1}^{P} \epsilon(S^\mu, S^{*\mu}) \quad \text{with} \quad S^\mu = \text{sign}[\mathbf{w} \cdot \boldsymbol{\xi}^\mu], \quad S^{*\mu} = \text{sign}[\mathbf{w}^* \cdot \boldsymbol{\xi}^\mu]. \quad (9)$$

With the binary error measure of Eq. (6), the cost function represents the number of disagreements between student and teacher for a given data set.

Without referring to a particular training prescription we can describe the outcome of suitable stochastic procedures in terms of a Gibbs-Boltzmann density of weight vectors

$$P_{eq}(\mathbf{w}) = \frac{e^{-\beta H(\mathbf{w})}}{Z} \quad \text{with} \quad Z = \int d\mu(\mathbf{w}) \, e^{-\beta H(\mathbf{w})}. \quad (10)$$

It describes a canonical ensemble of trained networks in thermal equilibrium at formal inverse temperature $\beta = 1/T$. The cost function $E(\mathbf{w})$ plays the role of the energy of state $\mathbf{w}$ and the normalization Z is known as the partition function. The measure $d\mu(\mathbf{w})$ is implicitly understood to incorporate restrictions of the N-dimensional integration such as the normalization $\mathbf{w}^2 = N$. Similarly, Z can be written as a sum over all possible weight configurations for systems with $\mathbf{w} \in \{-1, +1\}^N$.

In the limit $\beta \to \infty, T \to 0$, only the groundstate with minimal energy can be observed in the ensemble, as any other state will have an exponentially smaller P_{eq}. On the contrary, for $\beta \to 0, T \to \infty$, the energy becomes irrelevant and every state P_{eq} can occur with the same probability. In general, the parameter β controls the mean energy of the system which can be written as a thermal average of the form

$$\langle H \rangle_\beta = \int d\mu(\mathbf{w})\, H(\mathbf{w}) \frac{e^{-\beta H(\mathbf{w})}}{Z} = -\frac{\partial}{\partial \beta} \ln Z. \tag{11}$$

Quite generally, thermal averages can be written as appropriate derivatives of the so-called free energy $F = -\frac{1}{\beta} \ln Z$, which is also in the center of the following analysis. Introducing the microcanonical entropy $S(E)$ we can rewrite

$$Z = \int dE\, e^{-\beta E + S(E)} \quad \text{where} \quad S(E) = \ln \int d\mu(\mathbf{w})\, \delta[H(\mathbf{w}) - E] \tag{12}$$

with the Dirac delta-function $\delta[\ldots]$. For large systems in the thermodynamic limit $N \to \infty$ we assume that entropy and energy are extensive, i.e. that $S = N s$ and $E = N e$ with $e, s = \mathcal{O}(1)$. A saddle-point integration yields

$$\lim_{N \to \infty} (-\ln Z / N) = \beta F / N = \beta e - s(e) \tag{13}$$

where the right hand side $\beta F / N$ has to be evaluated in its minimum with respect to e for a given β.

2.5   Disorder Average and High-Temperature Limit

The consideration of a formal thermal equilibrium in the previous section refers to a particular data set $\mathbb{D}$, since the energy function $H(\mathbf{w})$ is defined with respect to the given example data. In order to obtain typical results independent of the particularities of a specific data set, an additional average over randomly generated $\mathbb{D}$ has to be performed.

In the simplest case, we consider data sets which comprise P independent vectors $\boldsymbol{\xi}^\mu$ with i.i.d. components that obey (4). Hence the corresponding density factorizes over examples $\mu = 1, 2, \ldots P$ and components $j = 1, 2, \ldots N$ of the feature vectors in $\mathbb{D}$.

The randomness in $\mathbb{D}$ can be interpreted as an external disorder which determines the actual energy function $H(\mathbf{w})$ and the corresponding thermal equilibrium. In addition to the thermal average discussed in the previous section, the associated quenched average is denoted as $\langle \ldots \rangle_{\mathbb{D}}$. Quantities of interest have to be studied in terms of appropriate averages of the form $\langle \langle \ldots \rangle_\beta \rangle_{\mathbb{D}}$ which can be derived from the quenched free energy

$$\langle F \rangle_{\mathbb{D}} = - \langle \ln Z \rangle_{\mathbb{D}} / \beta.$$

The computation of $\langle \ln Z \rangle_{\mathbb{D}}$ is, in general, quite involved and requires the application of sophisticated methods such as the replica trick [1,15,20–22].

We refrain from discussing the conceptual difficulties and mathematical subtleties of the replica approach. Instead we resort to a very much simplifying limit, which has been presented and discussed in [22]. In the extreme setting of learning at high formal temperature with $\beta \to 0$, the so-called annealed approximation

$$\langle \ln Z \rangle_{\mathbb{D}} \approx \ln \langle Z \rangle_{\mathbb{D}}$$

becomes exact and can be exploited to obtain the typical training outcome [20–22]. Note that in this limit also

$$\langle Z \rangle_{\mathbb{D}} = \left\langle \int d\mu(\mathbf{w}) e^{-\beta H(\mathbf{w})} \right\rangle_{\mathbb{D}} = \int d\mu(\mathbf{w}) e^{-\beta \langle H(\mathbf{w}) \rangle_{\mathbb{D}}} \quad \text{with}$$

$$\langle H(\mathbf{w}) \rangle_{\mathbb{D}} = \sum_{\mu=1}^{P} \left\langle \epsilon(S^\mu, S^{*\mu}) \right\rangle_{\mathbb{D}} = P \langle \epsilon_g . \rangle_{\mathbb{D}}. \tag{14}$$

Here we make use of the fact that the i.i.d. random examples in $\mathbb{D}$ contribute the same average error which is given by ϵ_g. It is expressed as a function of the order parameter R in Eq. (8). We can now perform a saddle point integration in analogy to Eqs. (12, 13) to obtain

$$\lim_{N \to \infty} (-\ln \langle Z \rangle_{\mathbb{D}} / N) = \beta \langle F \rangle_{\mathbb{D}} / N = \frac{\beta P}{N} \epsilon_g(R) - s(R). \tag{15}$$

Again, the right hand side has to be evaluated in its minimum, now with respect to the characteristic order parameter R of the system. The entropy term

$$s(R) = \frac{1}{N} \ln \int d\mu(\mathbf{w}) \delta[\mathbf{w} \cdot \mathbf{w}^* - NR] \tag{16}$$

can be obtained analytically by an additional saddle point integration making use of the integral representation of the δ-function [1,20–22]. Since $s(R)$ depends on potential constraints on the weight vectors as represented by $d\mu(\mathbf{w})$, we postpone the computation to the following sections.

In order to obtain meaningful results from the minimization with respect to R in Eq. (15), we have to assume that the number of examples P scales like

$$P = \alpha N / \beta \quad \text{with} \quad \alpha = \mathcal{O}(1). \tag{17}$$

Obviously, P should be proportional to the number N of adaptive weights in the system, which is consistent with an extensive energy. In addition, P has to

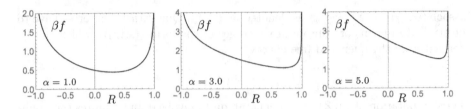

Fig. 1. The quenched free energy βf as a function of the order parameter R in the training scenario with spherical student and teacher perceptron, cf. Sect. 2.6. From left to right, the rescaled numbers of examples are $\alpha = 1.0, 3.0$ and 5.0, respectively.

grow like β^{-1} in the high temperature limit. The weak role of the energy in this limit has to be compensated for by an increased number of example data. In layman's terms: *"Almost nothing is learned from infinitely many examples"*. This also makes plausible the identification of the energy with the generalization error. The space of possible input vectors is sampled so well that training set performance and generalization behavior become indistinguishable.

Finally, the quenched free energy per weight, $f = \langle F \rangle_{\mathbb{D}}/N$ of the perceptron model in the high temperature limit has the form

$$\beta f = \alpha\, \epsilon_g(R) - s(R), \tag{18}$$

where α plays the role of an effective temperature parameter, which couples the number of examples and the formal temperature of the training process. These quantities cannot be varied independently within the simplifying limit $\beta \to 0$ in combination with $P/N \propto \beta^{-1}$.

2.6   Two Concrete Examples

Despite the significant simplifications and scaling assumptions, it is possible to obtain non-trivial, interesting results also in the high temperature limit. Very often, more sophisticated approaches, such as the replica method or the annealed approximation for finite training temperatures, confirm the results for $\beta \to 0$ qualitatively. Therefore, the simplified treatment has often been used to obtain first, useful insights into the qualitative properties of various learning scenarios. In this brief review, we restrict the discussion to two well-known results for simple model situations. Both concern the training of a simple perceptron in a student teacher scenario. Originally the models were treated in [22] and they have been revisited in several reviews, for instance, [20, 21]. We reproduce the results here as particularly illustrative examples for the statistical physics approach to learning.

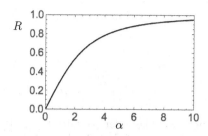 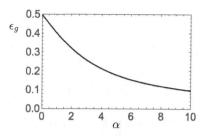

Fig. 2. Typical learning curves of the perceptron with continuous weights in the student teacher scenario, see Sect. 2.6. The left panel shows $R(\alpha)$, the right panel displays the corresponding generalization error $\epsilon_g(\alpha)$.

The Perceptron with Continuous Weights

Here we consider a student teacher scenario where the student weight vector $\mathbf{w} \in \mathbb{R}^N$ is normalized ($\mathbf{w}^2 = N$) but otherwise unrestricted.

The generalization error as a function of the student teacher overlap R is given in Eq. (8). The corresponding entropy, Eq. (16), can be obtained by means of a saddle point integration. Alternatively, one can interpret $e^N s$ as the volume of an $(N-1)$-dimensional hypersphere in weight space with radius $\sqrt{1-R^2}$, see [21] for the geometrical argument. One obtains

$$s(R) = \frac{1}{2} \ln(1 - R^2) + const., \tag{19}$$

where the additive constant does not depend on R. Apart from such irrelevant terms, we obtain the quenched free energy in the limit $\beta \to 0$ as

$$\beta f = \alpha \frac{1}{\pi} \arccos R - \frac{1}{2} \ln(1 - R^2). \tag{20}$$

In absence of training data, $\alpha = 0$, the maximum of the entropy term in $R = 0$ governs the behavior of the system. In the high-dimensional feature space, the student weight vector is expected to be orthogonal to the unknown $\mathbf{w}^*$.

The free energy is displayed in Fig. 1 for three different values of α. As α is increased, we observe that the minimum of βf is found in larger, positive values of R, reflecting the knowledge about the rule as inferred from the set of examples.

The student teacher overlap $R(\alpha)$ that corresponds to the minimum of βf is displayed in Fig. 2 (left panel). In this simple case, it can be obtained analytically from the necessary condition for the presence of a minimum:

$$\frac{\partial \beta f}{\partial R} = 0 \quad \Rightarrow \quad R(\alpha) = \frac{\alpha}{\sqrt{\alpha^2 + \pi^2}}. \tag{21}$$

By means of Eq. (8) this result translates into a learning curve $\epsilon_g(\alpha)$, which is shown in the right panel of Fig. 2. One can show that large training sets facilitate perfect generalization with

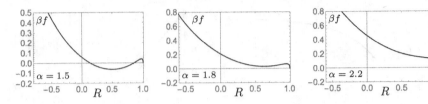

Fig. 3. The quenched free energy βf as a function of the order parameter R in the training scenario with Ising student and teacher perceptron, cf. Sect. 2.6. In the leftmost panel the rescaled numbers of examples is $\alpha = 1.5 < \alpha_c$, where $R = 1$ constitutes a local minimum while a state with $0 < R < 1$ is thermodynamically stable. In the center panel with $\alpha = 1.8 > \alpha_c$, here perfect generalization with $R = 1$ corresponds to the global minimum. The rightmost panel displays βf for $\alpha = 2.2 > \alpha_d$ where $R = 1$ constitutes its only minimum.

$$R(\alpha) \approx 1 - \frac{\pi^2}{2\alpha^2} \text{ and } \epsilon_g(\alpha) \approx \frac{1}{\alpha} \text{ for } \alpha \to \infty. \tag{22}$$

It is interesting to note that the basic asymptotic α-dependences are recovered in the more sophisticated application of the annealed approximation or the replica formalism [22]. Obviously, an explicit temperature dependence and the correct prefactors cannot be obtained in the simplifying limit.

The Perceptron with Discrete Weights

As an interesting exercise we also revisit the model with discrete student weights [22]. The term Ising perceptron has been coined for the model with weights $\mathbf{w} \in \{-1, 1\}^N$ [21,22]. Note that the assumed normalization $\mathbf{w}^2 = N$ is trivially satisfied. Moreover, the generalization error is also given by Eq. (8) since its derivation does not depend on details of the weight space.

The corresponding entropy can be obtained by a simple counting argument: In order to obtain an overlap $\sum_j w_j w_j^* = NR$, a number of $N(R+1)/2$ components must satisfy $w_j = w_j^*$ while for $N(R-1)/2$ we have $w_j = -w_j^*$. The associated entropy of mixing is given by the familiar form

$$s(R) = -\left(\frac{1+R}{2}\right) \ln \left(\frac{1+R}{2}\right) - \left(\frac{1-R}{2}\right) \ln \left(\frac{1-R}{2}\right). \tag{23}$$

The resulting free energy (18) as a function of R is displayed in Fig. 3 for three different values of α.

For all $\alpha > 0$, βf displays a local minimum in $R = 1$ with $f(R = 1) = 0$. For small α, however, a deeper minimum can be found with an overlap $0 < R < 1$. This is exemplified for $\alpha = 1.5$ in the leftmost panel of Fig. 3. The global minimum of βf determines the thermodynamically stable state of the system.

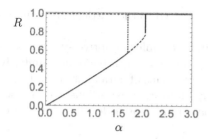
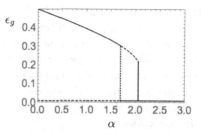

Fig. 4. Learning of the Ising perceptron with discrete weights in the student teacher scenario, see Sect. 2.6. The left panel shows $R(\alpha)$, the right panel displays the corresponding generalization error $\epsilon_g(\alpha)$. States corresponding to local minima of βf are marked by dashed lines, while solid lines mark the thermodynamically stable global minima. Vertical dotted and solid lines correspond to the critical $\alpha_c \approx 1.69$ and $\alpha_d \approx 2.08$, respectively.

For training sets with α larger than a critical value $\alpha_c \approx 1.69$, the state with $R = 1$ constitutes the global minimum. A competing configuration with $R < 1$ persists as a local minimum, but becomes unstable for $\alpha > \alpha_d \approx 2.08$, see the center and rightmost panel of Fig. 3.

The learning curves $R(\alpha)$ and $\epsilon_g(\alpha)$ reflect the specific α-dependence of βf in terms of a discontinuous phase transition. In Fig. 4, the solid lines mark the thermodynamically stable state in terms of $R(\alpha)$ (left panel) and $\epsilon_g(\alpha)$ (right panel). Dashed lines correspond to local minima of βf and the characteristic values α_c and α_d are marked by the dotted and solid vertical lines, respectively.

The essential findings of the high temperature treatment do carry over to the training at lower formal temperatures, qualitatively [21,22]. Most notably, the system displays a freezing transition to perfect generalization. Furthermore, the first order phase transition scenario will have non-trivial effects in practical training. The existence of metastable, poorly generalizing states can delay the success of training significantly. Related hysteresis effects with varying α have been observed in Monte Carlo simulations of the training process, see [21] and references therein.

3 Summary and Conclusion

This brief review merely discusses one goal of the statistical physics of learning: the computation of typical learning curves in clear-cut model scenarios. This type of results provide basic insight into relevant mechanisms and phenomena which play a role in practical machine learning setups as well. The framework provides a workshop in which to analyse, put forward and optimize training algorithms. Moreover it offers the possibility to systematically compare different adaptive systems, network architectures etc.

The classical examples discussed in this short tutorial concern merely the simplest models, i.e. the learning of a linearly separable rule with a percetpron network. The presentation is furthermore restricted to the particularly simplifying limit of training at high temperature.

In the literature, numerous studies of more complex adaptive systems, such as layered neural networks or support vector machines can be found. Similarly, models of unsupervised learning and related problems of data analysis and inference have been analysed. Among the many interesting extensions, we mention only the study of symmetry breaking phase transitions in feedforward layered neural networks.

The analysis of more realistic training at low formal temperatures requires a much more involved mathematical treatment. A thorough discussion thereof would be clearly beyond the scope of this brief introduction to the field. Indeed, the theory of learning has had a very fruitful impact on the development and understanding of sophisticated methods for the analysis of disordered systems in general.

Apart from the equilibrium approach discussed here, statistical physics also provides the tools to analyse non-equilibrium situations. This has helped to study the dynamics of learning in a very similar fashion. The resulting insights directly link to popular practical training prescriptions such as the popular stochastic gradient descent.

Recently, the statistical physics of learning is being rediscovered and has gained popularity again in the context of deep learning. A better theoretical understanding of this successful machine learning framework is highly desirable. Currently, many researchers revisit the statistical physics perspective to learning, aiming a fundamental insights into design and performance of, for instance, deep layered networks. A brief discussion of recent developments, challenges and open questions, as well as further references can be found in [32].

The author is convinced that the revival of the area will contribute significantly to the further development of machine learning and data analysis in general.

References

1. Hertz, J., Krogh, A., Palmer, R.G.: Introduction to the Theory of Neural Computation. Addison-Wesley (1991)
2. Hastie, T., Tibshirani, R., Friedman, J.: The Elements of Statistical Learning. SSS, Springer, New York (2009). https://doi.org/10.1007/978-0-387-84858-7
3. Bishop, C.: Pattern Recognition and Machine Learning. Cambridge University Press, Cambridge (2007)
4. Goodfellow, I., Bengio, Y., Courville, A.: Deep Learning. MIT Press (2016)
5. LeCun, Y., Bengio, Y., Hinton, G.: Deep learning. Nature **521**, 436–444 (2015)
6. Schmidhuber, J.: Deep learning in neural networks: an overview. Neural Netw. **61**, 85–117 (2015)
7. Saitta, L., Giordana, A., Cornuéjols, A.: Phase Transitions in Machine Learning, 383 p. Cambridge University Press (2011)
8. Rynkiewicz, J.: Asymptotic statistics for multilayer perceptrons with ReLU hidden units. In: Verleysen, M. (ed.) Proceedings European Symposium on Artificial Neural Networks (ESANN), 6 p. d-side publishing (2018)

9. Marcus, G.: Deep learning: a critical appraisal. http://arxiv.org/abs/1801.00631. Accessed 23 Apr 2018
10. Zhang, C., Bengio, S., Hardt, M., Recht, B., Vinyals, O.: Understanding deep learning requires rethinking generalization. In: Proceedings of the 6th International Conference on Learning Representations ICLR (2017)
11. Martin, C.H., Mahoney, M.W.: Rethinking generalization requires revisiting old ideas: statistical mechanics approaches and complex learning behavior. Computing Research Repository CoRR, eprint 1710.09553 (2017).http://arxiv.org/abs/1710.09553
12. Lin, H.W., Tegmark, M., Rolnick, D.: Why does deep and cheap learning work so well? J. Stat. Phys. **168**(6), 1223–1247 (2017)
13. Erhan, D., Bengio, Y., Courville, A., Manzagol, P.-A., Vincent, P.: Why does unsupervised pre-training help deep learning? J. Mach. Learn. Res. **11**, 625–660 (2010)
14. Metropolis, N., Rosenbluth, A.W., Rosenbluth, M.N., Teller, A.H., Teller, E.: Equations of state calculations by fast computing machines. J. Chem. Phys. **21**, 1087 (1953)
15. Mezard, M., Parisi, G., Virasoro, M.: Spin Glass Theory and Beyond. World Scientific (1986)
16. Hopfield, J.J.: Neural networks and physical systems with emergent collective computational abilities. Proc. Nat. Acad. Sci. USA **79**(8), 2554–2558 (1982)
17. Amit, D.J., Gutfreund, H., Sompolinsky, H.: Storing infinite numbers of patterns in a spin-glass model of neural networks. Phys. Rev. Lett. **55**(14), 1530–1533 (1985)
18. Gardner, E.: Maximum storage capacity in neural networks. Europhys. Lett. **4**(4), 481–486 (1988)
19. Gardner, E.: The space of interactions in neural network models. J. Phys. A Math. General **21**(1), 257–270 (1988)
20. Engel, A., Van den Broeck, C.: Statistical Mechanics of Learning, 342 p. Cambridge University Press (2001)
21. Watkin, T.L.H., Rau, A., Biehl, M.: The statistical mechanics of learning a rule. Rev. Mod. Phys. **65**(2), 499–556 (1993)
22. Seung, H.S., Sompolinsky, H., Tishby, N.: Statistical mechanics of learning from examples. Phys. Rev. A **45**, 6065–6091 (1992)
23. Kinzel, W.: Phase transitions of neural networks. Philos. Mag. B **77**(5), 1455–1477 (1998)
24. Opper, M.: Learning and generalization in a two-layer neural network: the role of the Vapnik-Chervonenkis dimension. Phys. Rev. Lett. **72**, 2113 (1994)
25. Herschkowitz, D., Opper, M.: Retarded learning: rigorous results from statistical mechanics. Phys. Rev. Lett. **86**, 2174 (2001)
26. Goldt, S., Mézard, M., Krzakala, F., Zdeborová, L.: Modelling the influence of data structure on learning in neural networks. eprint 1909.11500v1[stat.ML] (2019). http://arxiv.org/abs/1909.11500
27. Cocco, S., Monasson, R., Posani, L., Rosay, S., Tubiana, J.: Statistical physics and representations in real and artificial neural networks. Phys. A Stat. Mech. Its Appl. **504**, 45–76 (2018)
28. Kadmon, J., Sompolinsky, H.: Optimal architectures in a solvable model of deep networks. In: Lee, D.D. Sugiyama, M., Luxburg, U.V., Guyon, I., Garnett, R. (eds.) Advances in Neural Information Processing Systems (NIPS 29), pp. 4781–4789. Curran Associates Inc. (2016)

29. Dauphin, Y., Pascanu, R., Gulcehre, C., Cho, K., Ganguli, S., Bengio, Y.: Identifying and attacking the saddle point problem in high-dimensional non-convex optimization. In: Ghahramani, Z., Welling, M., Cortes, C., Lawrence, N.D., Weinberger, K.Q. (eds.) Advances in Neural Information Processing Systems (NIPS 27), pp. 2933–2941. Curran Associates Inc. (2014)
30. Pankaj, M., Lang, A.H., Schwab, D.: An exact mapping from the variational renormalization group to deep learning. arXiv repository [stat.ML], eprint 1410.3831v1 (2014). https://arxiv.org/abs/1410.3831v1
31. Sohl-Dickstein, J., et al.: Deep unsupervised learning using non-equilibrium thermodynamics. Proc. Mach. Learn. Res. **37**, 2256–2265 (2016)
32. Biehl, M., Caticha, N., Opper, M., Villmann, T.: Statistical physics of learning and inference. In: Verleysen, M. (ed.) Proceedings European Symposium on Artificial Neural Networks (ESANN), pp. 501–509. d-side Publishing (2019)

Emotion Mining: from Unimodal
to Multimodal Approaches

Chiara Zucco, Barbara Calabrese, and Mario Cannataro$^{(\boxtimes)}$

Data Analytics Research Center, Department of Medical and Surgical Sciences,
University "Magna Græcia" of Catanzaro, Catanzaro, Italy
{chiara.zucco,calabreseb,cannataro}@unicz.it

Abstract. In the last decade, Sentiment Analysis and Affective Computing have found applications in different domains. In particular, the interest of extracting emotions in healthcare is demonstrated by the various applications which encompass patient monitoring and adverse events prediction. Thanks to the availability of large datasets, most of which are extracted from social media platforms, several techniques for extracting emotion and opinion from different modalities have been proposed, using both unimodal and multimodal approaches. After introducing the basic concepts related to emotion theories, mainly borrowed from social sciences, the present work reviews three basic modalities used in emotion recognition, i.e. textual, audio and video, presenting for each of these i) some basic methodologies, ii) some among the widely used datasets for the training of supervised algorithms and iii) briefly discussing some deep Learning architectures. Furthermore, the paper outlines the challenges and existing resources to perform a multimodal emotion recognition which may improve performances by combining at least two unimodal approaches. architecture to perform multimodal emotion recognition.

Keywords: Sentiment analysis · Affective computing · Text mining · Data mining · Neuroscience · Hardware accelerators

1 Introduction

Affect is a term widely used in psychology to describe the psychophysiological response to stimuli, as for example emotions, while the word sentiment refers to a more organized and highly socialized feeling, which can be summarized with the expression "an opinion colored by emotion" [1].

Several are the studies showing how affective phenomena may influence different human cognitive processes such as the mechanisms of attention and information processing, as well as the processes of judgment and decision making [2] and communication. On the other hand, it is well known how many pathological conditions, as for example mood disorders, are characterized by a distorted and inconsistent emotional state [3,4].

© The Author(s) 2021
K. Amunts et al. (Eds.): BrainComp 2019, LNCS 12339, pp. 143–158, 2021.
https://doi.org/10.1007/978-3-030-82427-3_11

In humans the ability to be aware, to express and to recognize their own and other's emotions through communicative processes is more developed than in other animals. This outstanding capacity reflects the additional hierarchical levels of processing. Levels that allow learning, inference and simulation [5] and which may constitute a crucial aspect in emulating human intelligence [6]. The development of computational models capable of mimic the natural ability to identify emotional states from speech, facial expressions and written messages is a challenging topic which is gaining particular interest in recent years. The main areas for the computational study related to the recognition of emotions are Affective Computing and Sentiment Analysis. Historically, Affective Computing relates to the area of Artificial Intelligence (AI) that aims at the development of systems capable of recognizing, interpreting and simulating emotions understood in the meaning of affect, and therefore the detection of affective human states is more focused on different biosignals, while Sentiment Analysis aims at extracting opinions and emotions in the sense of sentiment, and was mainly focused on textual sources.

As a result of the popularity of social platforms, the availability of heterogeneous content related to opinions and emotions is increasingly growing, offering the possibility to collect and merge the multimodal information for knowledge extraction. Since communication among human is a mix of verbal and nonverbal content, a system able to measure the emotional state of a person would take advantage from a multimodal approach. For this reason, lately different efforts in performing multimodal emotion recognition have been made.

Even though significant AI advancements, the topic continues to pose numerous open challenges both in the field of research and in large industrial sectors, due to the significant impact on marketing strategies [7], recommender systems [8] and, recently, also in the medical and psychological field for the development of diagnostic and therapeutic clinical decision support systems [9, 10].

The present work aims to provide a general overview of the technologies and methodologies involved in recognition of emotional states and to give an insight into the opportunity and challenges for developing an emotion recognition system that merges different modalities. The paper is organized as follows: in Sect. 2 the fundamental and most accepted approaches for the scientific study of emotions in psychological, cognitive and social science are presented. Section 3 is devoted to discuss the basic unimodal approaches used in emotion recognition, and also to present some existing datasets and used tools. Section 4 discusses the use of Deep Learning (DL) in emotion recognition. In Sect. 5 the opportunities and challenges which arises in developing a multimodal emotion recognition system are outlined. Finally, Sect. 6 concludes the paper.

2   Emotion Theories

The difficulty of defining emotions in scientific terms is a well-known problem in the history of psychology. Currently, there is no scientific consensus on the definition of emotion, but there are several heuristic theories which can be grouped into two different viewpoints: the "basic emotions" and the "appraisal" approaches[2]. Despite the variability of the emotional responses, which may be linked to subjective, cognitive and cultural differences, basic emotions models presuppose the existence of universal and easily recognizable psychophysiological states.

The main assumption underlying the basic emotions approach [11,12], is that emotions belonging to the same class may vary in intensity or other dimensions, but share not only comparable causes and stimuli of responses but also have a biological analogy, as for example similar behavioral patterns, bodily activations and facial expressions. This strands tends to identify this set of similar emotions with the most prototypical one (for example "joy" contains "happiness", "enjoyment", "pleasure", "joyfulness", "ecstasy", "thrill" etc.) [13].

On the other hand, appraisal approaches [14–16] assume that emotions are triggered by a physiological response which, unlike the basic emotions approach, derives from an interpretation of the specific situation through personal criteria [13]. With respect to the identification and classification of emotions, there is a tendency to differentiate between discrete and dimensional theories of emotions. A short description of these models will be given below.

2.1   Discrete Theories of Emotions

The models of discrete emotions are generally the most used in the field of Affective Computing, especially as regards the recognition of emotions from facial expressions. Numerous models of discrete basic human emotions exist, differing among each other in the number and the type of identified emotions. Some widespread criteria to identify basic emotions from non-basic ones are: 1) a universally recognizable facial expression, 2) a rapid spontaneous and automatic recognition, 3) a unique feeling [11]. To date, the most accredited models of discrete emotions in the scientific community refer to the theories of Arnold, Ekman, Izard, Oatley and Johnson-Laird, Plutchik and Tomkins. Table 1 summarizes the list of basic emotions for each of these theories.

Table 1. Emotions definitions.

Categorical emotion theory	Identified emotions
Arnold [17]	Anger, aversion, courage, dejection, desire, despair, fear, hate, hope, love, sadness
Ekman [11]	Anger, disgust, fear, joy, sadness, surprise
Izard [12]	Anger, contempt, disgust, distress, fear, guilt, interest, joy, shame, surprise
Oatley and Johnson-Laird [18]	Anger, disgust, anxiety, happiness, sadness
Plutchik [19]	Acceptance, anger, anticipation, disgust, joy, fear, sadness, surprise
Tomkins [20]	Anger, interest, contempt, disgust, distress, fear, joy, shame, surprise

Among the theories summarized in the Table 1, the one proposed by Oatley and Johnson-Laird [18] has the difference that the existence of basic emotions not only has biological foundations but also a semantic component. The authors address basic emotions as "semantic primitives", which means that humans know they are feeling a particular emotion X but they don't know how to define it.

In [21], an interesting work related to the evaluation of emotion theories for computational purposes is carried out. In particular, starting from a corpus of over 21,000 tweets, six basic emotions theories were analyzed through an iterative clustering algorithm based on a variant of Latent Semantic Analysis to discern which one has the most semantically distinct set of emotions. Results showed that Ekman's model, which is the most popular in Affective Computing, is the one in which emotions are more semantically distinct. Then, Bann et al. [21] also considered 21 emotions given by joining all the six different models and extracted the optimal semantically separated basic emotion set which was proposed as a new model of basic emotions consisting of eight emotions: Accepting, Ashamed, Contempt, Interested, Joyful, Pleased, Sleepy, Stressed.

2.2 Dimensional Emotional Models

Although the most accredited paradigm in the field of neuroscience research states that emotions can be divided into discrete and independent categories, numerous dimensional models were proposed in the literature. In dimensional theories take as and assumption that all the affective states derive from common neurophysiological systems. Consequently, every emotion can be expressed as a combination of these systems, also addressed as dimensions. Only a few are the dimensional theories widely accepted by the scientific community, described below.

The complex model of emotions of Russell [22] is one of the first and most well-known dimensional models. The complex model identifies two independent dimensions: valence and arousal, represented as the two dimensions of a plane in which 28 emotions are mapped in a circle. The arousal-nonaraousal scale measures the intensity of emotion and constitutes the vertical axis of the representation system. The points belonging to the upper semicircle are characterized by high arousal, while the points belonging to the inferior semicircumference are characterized by low arousal. Valence is measured by a pleasure-displeasure scale, which measures the pleasure of an emotion. On the left semicircumference, unpleasant emotions are represented, while on the right semi-circumference pleasant emotions are shown [19].

Furthermore there are hybrid models, for example the Plutchik model is an example of a model that merges the categorical and dimensional approaches. In fact the Plutchik basic emotions represented in Table 1 only refer to the primary Plutchik's emotions. In fact, in his model, named "Wheel of emotions", affective states are represented in a structural and circocentric way. The proximity to the center represents a greater intensity, while the eight dimensions identified are visually represented as eight sectors inscribed in the circocentric structure and arranged as four pairs of opposites: Joy-Sadness, Fear-Anger, Anticipation-Surprise, Disgust-Trust.

3 Basic Unimodal Emotion Recognition Approaches

The focus of this Section is to present the three most used modalities for the recognition of emotions: text, images and audio. For each of the modality, the main tasks, the existing approaches, the available datasets and the functionalities of some existing tools in the literature will be presented. We term those methods as "unimodal" because each one uses only a type of input data to detect emotions.

3.1 Emotion Recognition from Textual Sources

As stated in Sect. 1, in general extracting opinions and emotions from textual content refers to the area known as Sentiment Analysis which may be seen as the intersection of statistical methods, Machine Learning, Information Retrieval and Natural Language Processing.

In the foundational works of Liu, a computational definition of emotion end sentiment is presented [23] and to date it is widely accepted among the Sentiment Analysis research community.

According to his definition, an opinion is a quintuple (entity, entity's feature, sentiment, opinion holder, time) and the most basic Sentiment Analysis task is polarity detection, whose main goal is to detect whether a text unit contains a positive, negative, or neutral opinion, and/or also considering a "valence" score, indicating how strongly T is positive or negative. Valence scores can be expressed as a nominal (strong negative, weak negative, weak positive, strong positive), or as a continuous variable, frequently belonging to a specific range (for example $[-1, 1]$). Similarly, an emotion can be seen as a quintuple in which sentiment is replaced with an emotion type. More in details, a categorical emotion type may be expressed as the couple (emotion class, emotion intensity), where:

- the emotion class indicates the class to which the specific emotion belongs w.r.t. a given system of basic emotions representation;
- the emotion intensity represents a "valence" score, indicating how strongly the emotion is expressed in the given text unit.

When considering a discrete theory of emotions, a basic emotion detection task in SA can be seen as the multiclass classification problem that, given an input text T and a list $E = [E_1, \cdots, E_k]$ of basic emotions classes, aims at detecting whether the text T contains one emotion E_i for $i = 1 \cdots k$ and, eventually extracting the respective valence score v_i. However, as will be shown in the following Subsection, existing annotated emotion datasets do not contain only basic emotions and therefore the classification problem usually is designed as a multiclass and multilabel problem. If instead a dimensional theory of emotions is taken into account, a basic emotion detection task may be seen as the regression problem of assigning valence or arousal values to a text T, on the basis of its content.

A SA process generally follows a standard Text Mining process. Input data are extracted from social media, or other sources converted in plain text format and pre-processed. Pre-processing methods include standard NLP and text mining techniques such as stemming, tokenization, part of speech tagging, entity extraction and relation extraction. For an online text, specific data pre-processing methods include cleaning, like removing URLs, HTML tags, abbreviation expansion, emoji, and repeated characters handling. The intermediate step of a Sentiment Analysis process is represented by the analysis module that can follow three types of approaches, that is, supervised, unsupervised and hybrid approach and it is based on three possible levels of analysis, i.e., document-based, sentence-based and aspect-based [24–26].

In lexicon based approaches, the starting point is a set of words in which for every term a given emotion or relative polarity is associated, with or without a score. This set of words can be manually expanded through the use of synonyms or antonyms following a dictionary-based approach. A major issue of lexicon based approaches is to not take into account the specific application domain, with a resulting low text-contextualization capability. Also statistical and semantic methods have been used to enrich the set of annotated words, following a so called corpus-based approach. Despite having the advantage that the performance does not depend on the size of the dataset, as in machine learning approaches, a significant drawback in lexicon-based approach is that it is not suitable for the rapid change to which the language of the web is subject. To exploit the advantages of the two previous approaches, hybrid methodologies that combine machine learning techniques with lexicon-based approaches have been developed.

3.1.1 Available Textual Datasets

To identify the polarity/emotions of an input text, supervised methods need a set of annotated data on which the model is trained. One of the challenges in sentiment analysis is that polarity and emotions expressed in the text strongly depend on used language, context and domain.

Most of the datasets used within the SA are manually annotated. One of the problems related to manual annotation is that the human evaluation of "sentiment" is strongly conditioned by personal experiences, thoughts and beliefs. It is estimated that different people who read a text agree on the generic "sentiment" contained in it only in the 60–65% of cases on average. It is therefore clear how difficult it might be to obtain high quality datasets, reaching high values of "inter-annotation agreement" levels, especially in the case of recognition of emotions. However, the classification of polarity is the textual categorization task that currently holds the largest number of well-noted datasets. For this reason, in this section most of the datasets reported are mainly annotated to perform polarity detection. Few are the datasets that can be used as a benchmark for the evaluation of the performance of the classification algorithms.

- IMDb is a dataset of movie reviews collected from "Internet Movie Database" (IMDb). There are several versions of the dataset that have been collected and annotated. The most used versions are those noted at the document level. In particular, in the version of Pang and Lee [27], known as "Movie Review Dataset", there are 2000 reviews, 1000 categorized as positive and 1000 as negative. A second dataset (called "IMDb dataset") was annotated by Maas et al. [28] and consists of 50,000 movie reviews. Positive polarity is associated with the text of the review if the movie has been evaluated with more than six stars and negative polarity otherwise.
- Stanford Twitter Sentiment (STS), also known as Sentiment 140[1], is an annotated dataset introduced by Go et al. [29]. The training set contains 1.6 million tweets containing emoticons. The annotation was performed automatically by assigning a positive label to the tweet containing positive emoticons :), :-),:),: D, or =) and negative if it contains negative emoticons :(, :-(, o: (. However, since the emoticons may not reflect the actual sentiment of the tweet, the dataset has been extensively used for subjectivity classification tasks as well as a dataset for sentiment analysis.
- Sentiment Strength Twitter Dataset (SS-Tweet). Proposed by Thelwall et al. [30] for the evaluation of the SentiStrength tool , the dataset contains 4242 manually recorded tweets. Unlike the datasets described so far, the annotation is ordinal, in a range -5 (extremely negative) to 5 (extremely positive).
- SemEval Datasets: SemEval (Semantic Evaluation) is a series of computational competitions of semantic analysis systems taking place annually. The sentiment analysis task was introduced for the first time in SemEval-2013. The dataset has been annotated with the use of Amazon Mechanical Turk[2], for a total of 15196 tweets annotated for SA task at document and aspect level. The datasets from SemEval-2014 to SemEval-2016 are extensions of SemEval2013. In SemEval2016 the dataset has been extended to include other tasks, such as the quantification of tweets with the aim of estimating the distribution of tweets between classes compared to individual tweets. Finally, the SemEval-2017 and SemEval-2018 competitions were more focused on the categorization of affect in the Tweets. They are emotional datasets, scoring for a single emotion, rating for a single emotion, classification among 9 emotions and in addition the neutral class, scoring and valence rating (agreement of terms of positive or negative sentiment) [31].

3.2 Affective Computing Methodologies

A generic Affective Computing process starts with one or more biosignal acquisition. Typically these include measures related to physical aspects and physiological signals. Only the first category, whose standard modalities are facial or body expressions (such as gestures and movements) and speech will be discussed.

After this first step, a pre-processing of these signals is needed to remove or decrease the noise, that can be given, for example, by artifacts and, consequently,

---

[1] http://help.sentiment140.com/for-students.

[2] http://mturk.com.

increase the Ratio between Signal and Noise (SNR). Other pre-processing tasks are filtering and segmentation, concerning events or stimuli. A feature selection task can be applied to perform the analysis only on a reduced feature set.

Depending on the type of analysis to be performed, different features can be considered, for example, time (e.g., statistical analysis), frequency (e.g., Fourier analysis), time-frequency (e.g., wavelets), or power domain (e.g., periodogram and autoregression).

3.3 Emotion Recognition from Facial Expression

The foundational study in [32] reported that the 55% of the communication is visual. Therefore, expressions and body gestures are considered the most obvious and significant channels to infer affect. Ekman's theory of basic emotion [11] is the dominant emotion theory to classify facial expressions.

Each of the basic emotions is characterized by a series of muscular movements, formalized by what is called the Facial Action Coding System (FACS) and reported in Table 2. The Facial Action Code System (FACS) was published by Paul Ekman and Wallace Friesen in 1978 and, subsequently, updated in 1992 and again in 2002 [33]. The FACS was widely used for experiments on the recognition of emotions by the computer, from human facial expressions. This system objectively measures the frequency and intensity of facial expressions and deduces what is called an action unit (AU).

In order to provide a specific index for each type of movement and expression, the FACS takes into consideration 44 fundamental units named by Ekman and Friesen "Action Units AU" which can give rise to more than 7000 possible combinations. The total number of classified movements or characteristics is 58, some of which are typically associated with a specific emotion, while others are not associated with any other specific emotion.

Table 2. Description of facial expressions in relation to the six Ekman's basic emotions theory.

Emotion	Description of facial expression
Disgust	Curled nose, raised cheeks, raised upper lip, upper eyelid and lowered eyebrows, raised lower eyelid
Anger	Lowered eyebrows tending to join in the center, tensions in the upper and lower eyelids, pressed lips
Joy	Wrinkles around the eyes, upper lower eyelids and raised cheeks, corners of the mouth stretched upwards
Sadness	Inner angles of the raised eyebrows, inner angles of the upper eyelids raised, corners of the mouth downwards
Surprise	Eyebrows raised and bent upwards, eyes wide open, mouth open
Fear	Raised eyebrows that tend to unite, upper eyelid raised, lower eyelid stretched, mouth open and lips stretched outward

Some of the most important techniques for facial expression recognition are briefly described below:

- Active Appearance Models (AAM) [34]: they are well-known algorithms for modeling deformable objects. The models decouple the shape and texture of objects, using a gradient-based model adaptation approach. The most popular applications of AAM include recognition, tracking, segmentation and synthesis.
- Active Shape Models (ASM) [35]: these are statistical models that adapt to the data or object of an image in a manner consistent with the training data provided. These models are mainly used to improve the automatic analysis of images in noisy or messy environments.
- Muscle-based models [36]: these are models that consist of characteristic facial points corresponding to the facial muscles, for detecting the movement of facial components, such as the eyebrows, the eyes and the mouth, thus recognizing facial expressions.
- Constrained local 3D model (CLM-Z) [37] is a non-rigid face tracking model used to trace facial features in various poses, including both depth and intensity information. Non-rigid face tracking refers to points of interest in an image, such as the tip of the nose, the corners of the eyes and lips. The CLM-Z model can be described by the parameters $p = [s, R, q, t]$, where s is a scale factor, R is the rotation of the object, t represents the 2D translation and q is the vector that describes the non-rigid variation of the q.
- GAVAM (Generalized Adaptive View-Based Appearance Model) [38] is a probabilistic structure that combines dynamic or movement-based approaches to track the position and orientation of the head through video sequences and employs user-independent static approaches to detect the head position from an image. GAVAM is considered a real-time high-precision, user-independent algorithm for tracking the position of the head in real time.

3.4 Emotion Recognition from Speech

The analysis of expressive language consists in examining the paralinguistic characteristics, that is, the aspects of verbal and non-verbal communication, such as the tone of the voice and its intensity. The analysis can be conducted from different points of view, including signal processing, linguistics, psychoacoustics and speech recognition.

A first type of analysis is based on the construction of voice production models that try to model speech (speech) considering the breathing mechanisms and the structure of the phonatory apparatus (primarily vocal cords, mouth and nose). A second approach involves the study of speech from the point of view of perception that analyzes how speech is perceived and processed by the ear and the brain. The first approach, specifically, seeks to model the production of the item using mathematical models of the vocal tract. For the formulation of mathematical models, the vocal tract is studied by analyzing images of the vocal part obtained by ultrasonography, digital radiography and magnetic resonance.

Variations in the breathing pattern, specific vocal cord shape factors can determine variations in prosodic parameters, such as duration, intensity, fundamental frequency and spectral content of speech. Specifically, the fundamental frequency is the vibration speed of the vocal cords and depends on the size and tension of the vocal cords at a given instant of time. It can change in relation to stress, emotion and level of intonation.

In [39] and [40] the most relevant features for the recognition of emotions like the pitch contour, the energy of speech signals, and features related to spectral content are described. At the linguistic level, the analysis for the recognition of emotions involves the identification of the intonation of sentences, analysis of effort and accent in the pronunciation of words and sentences.

3.4.1 Existing Databases of Emotional Speech

- EMODB[3]: The Berlin Database of Emotional Speech (EMODB) is a public German speech database that incorporates audio files with seven emotions: happiness, sadness, anger, fear, disgust, boredom, and neutral [41].
- SAVEE[4]: The Surrey Audio-Visual Expressed Emotion (SAVEE) is a public British English speech database that has audio files with seven emotion labels: happiness, sadness, anger, fear, disgust, surprise, and neutral [42].
- EMOVO[5]: is a public Italian speech database that includes audio files with seven emotion labels: happiness, sadness, anger, fear, disgust, surprise, and neutral [43].

4 Deep Learning Algorithms for Emotion Detection

The performance of the emotion extraction approaches presented so far is strongly related to how data are represented. In this sense, an essential step is feature engineering, i.e., the process that uses domain knowledge to design a good representation of data in terms of suitable features. By taking advantage of the large training dataset, Deep Learning Algorithm seeks to learn data representation along with the mapping that associates each input representation to its output. Moreover, Deep Neural Networks (DNNs) are Artificial Neural Networks designed to have different levels of non-linear and nested operations, that have shown to improve non-linear model tasks. The previous statements are some of the key points explaining the popularity of Deep Neural Networks (DNNs) and why they have increasingly been implemented also to face the problem of emotion recognition, by achieving state-of-the-art results for a wide range of tasks [44, 45]. Several DNNs architectures have been proposed both in Sentiment Analysis and Affective Computing, for example, Convolutional Neural Networks (CNN) [46, 47], Recurrent Neural Networks (RNNs) with or without attention mechanism, Autoencoders [48] and also Deep Belief Networks (DBN) [48–50].

---

[3] http://emodb.bilderbar.info/start.html.

[4] http://personal.ee.surrey.ac.uk/Personal/P.Jackson/SAVEE/.

[5] http://voice.fub.it/activities/corpora/emovo/index.html.

Both in Sentiment Analysis and Affective Computing, a key role is played in capturing long-term dependencies intended for example as extracting relations among distant words in a sentence but also as capturing temporal variations in facial or vocal expressions. To address this problem, a particular set of RNNs model is typically used in a practical application and are called gated recurrent RNNs, in particular, Long Short Term Memory (LSTM) network [51]. For what concerns textual emotion recognition, LSTMs models are the state-of-the-art algorithm in time series predictions features, for example monitoring systems [52]. In Face emotion recognition, Gated RNNs have been combined with CNN to improve sequential images modelling [53].

5 Challenges and Tools for Multimodal Emotion Recognition

Recently, the scientific community has been increasing efforts for the joint application of Sentiment Analysis and Affective Computing techniques to create multi-modal systems, especially for monitoring and preventing mental health.

For example, in [54], a system that combines Sentiment Analysis and Affective Computing techniques to assess a subject's mental health is presented. In particular, the authors proposed the use of embedded sensors in mobile devices (such as laptops and smartphones) to trace head and eye movements, facial expressions as well as heartbeat. Among the features useful to verify interactions among users, the speed of typing, the number of clicks and mouse movements, etc. were considered, starting from the assumption that a positive or negative mood has effects on the different degrees of activity of the user. Lastly, the monitoring of sentiment associated with the text, related to user posts on Twitter, was performed using a free tool for sentiment analysis, i.e., *Sentiment 140*[6] and also a prediction algorithm for images posted along with tweets was used.

The major challenges for developing an integrated system, especially in combining data from integrated daily devices, can be identified in the following:

1. input data should be appropriate to the type of analysis to be made. For example, even if smartphones allow videos with good quality, the facial expression recognition process requires high-resolution images;
2. the choice of appropriate pre-processing, feature extraction and analysis techniques to achieve good performance is mandatory;
3. the selection of the most suitable approach for integrating information extracted from multiple sources in the system is crucial.

Concerning the last point, commonly used approaches are the following:

- Fusion at feature-level: after a first phase of pre-processing of data extracted from different sources, all features are considered as different components of a joined feature vector, and then classification is performed accordingly.

---

[6] http://www.sentiment140.com/.

- Fusion at decision level: instead of combining features in a single vector features as in feature-level fusion, a separate classifier for each modality is used. The output of each classifier was treated as a classification score.

In [55], both the previous approaches were tested for integrating facial expression, speech, and textual data to build a multi-modal sentiment analysis framework. The experimental results show that the accuracy of fusion at the feature level is higher than the accuracy of fusion at decision-level. Accurately, the authors reported a precision value of 78.2% and a recall value of 77.1% for tests relative to feature-level fusion, whereas they referred a precision value of 75.2% and a recall value of 73.4% for decision level fusion. Another remarkable point is that, regardless of the fusion techniques, the results show how the simultaneous use of video, text and audio modalities allows achieving better accuracy than when only pairs of the three patterns are considered. Considering the approach based on fusion at features level, the precision values of experiments are: (i) 72.45% by using only visual and text-based features, (ii) 73.21% by using visual and audio-based features and (iii) 71.15% by using audio and text-based features.

5.1 Existing Multimodal Dataset for Emotion Recognition

- SEMAINE Database. This dataset was developed in 2007 by McKeown et al. [56]. It is a large audiovisual database created for building agents capable of involving a person in a prolonged and emotional conversation using a Sensitive Artificial Listener (SAL) [57] paradigm. SAL is an interaction that involves two parts: a 'man' and an 'operator' (a machine or a person who simulates a machine). There were 150 participants, 959 conversations, each lasting 5 min. For the recordings, participants were asked to speak in turn to four emotionally stereotyped characters. The characters are Prudence, which is balanced and sensitive; Poppy, who is happy and outgoing; Spike, who is angry and in conflict; and Obadiah, who is sad and depressive.
- Interactive emotional dyadic acquisition database (IEMOCAP). The IEMO-CAP dataset was developed in 2008 by Busso et al. [58]. 10 actors were asked to record their facial expressions in front of the cameras. In particular, the dataset contains a total of 10 h of recording, each of which expresses one of the following emotions: happiness, anger, sadness, frustration and a neutral state.
- eNTERFACE. This dataset was developed in 2006 by Martin et al. [59] and contains audio and video for the evaluation of algorithms for the recognition of emotions from audio and video. The emotions labeled are: happiness, sadness, surprise, anger, disgust and fear.
- CK++ dataset: the Cohn Kanade dataset contains facial images of 210 adults. The participants are 18–50 years old, 81% Americans, 13% Afro Americans and 6% of other ethnic groups; 69% females. Participants are asked to perform 23 facial expressions.

- Belfast Database. This data set was developed in 2000 by Douglas-Cowie et al. [57]. The database consists of audiovisual data of people discussing emotional issues and are taken from television chat programs and religious programs. Includes 100 speakers and 239 clips, with 1 neutral clip and 1 emotional clip for each speaker. Two types of descriptors were provided for each clip: dimensional and categorical, according to the different emotion approaches.

6   Conclusions

This article presented an overview of the existing approaches for extracting sentiment and emotion from different input modalities through the use of Sentiment Analysis and Affective Computing techniques. In particular, audio, video and textual data were considered and, for each input modality a pipeline of analysis, existing datasets and tools were presented. Deep Learning approaches were also considered and discussed. Subsequently, recent efforts and challenges to combine these different unimodal approaches toward multimodal systems were reported.

References

1. Hockenbur, D., Hockenbur, S.: Discovering Psychology. Macmillan, London (2010)
2. Jeon, M.: Emotions and affect in human factors and human-computer interaction: Taxonomy, theories, approaches, and methods. In: Emotions and Affect in Human Factors and Human-Computer Interaction, pp. 3–26. Elsevier (2017)
3. Valstar, M.: Automatic behaviour understanding in medicine. In: Proceedings of the 2014 Workshop on Roadmapping the Future of Multimodal Interaction Research including Business Opportunities and Challenges, pp. 57–60. ACM (2014)
4. Zucco, C., Calabrese, B., Cannataro, M.: Sentiment analysis and affective computing for depression monitoring. In: 2017 IEEE International Conference on Bioinformatics and Biomedicine (BIBM), pp. 1988–1995. IEEE (2017)
5. Smith, R., Lane, R.D., Steklis, N., Weihs, K., Steklis, H.D.: The evolution and development of the uniquely human capacity for emotional awareness: a synthesis of comparative anatomical, cognitive, neurocomputational, and evolutionary psychological perspectives (2019)
6. Cambria, E., Das, D., Bandyopadhyay, S., Feraco, A.: A Practical Guide to Sentiment Analysis. Springer International Publishing, Cham (2017). https://doi.org/10.1007/978-3-319-55394-8
7. Atzeni, M., Dridi, A., Reforgiato Recupero, D.: Fine-grained sentiment analysis on financial microblogs and news headlines. In: Dragoni, M., Solanki, M., Blomqvist, E. (eds.) SemWebEval 2017. CCIS, vol. 769, pp. 124–128. Springer, Cham (2017). https://doi.org/10.1007/978-3-319-69146-6_11
8. Jayashree, R., Kulkarni, D.: Recommendation system with sentiment analysis as feedback component. In: Deep, K., et al. (eds.) Proceedings of Sixth International Conference on Soft Computing for Problem Solving. AISC, vol. 547, pp. 359–367. Springer, Singapore (2017). https://doi.org/10.1007/978-981-10-3325-4_36
9. Rosenquist, J.N., Fowler, J.H., Christakis, N.A.: Social network determinants of depression. Mol. Psychiatry 16(3), 273–281 (2011)

10. Coviello, L.L., et al.: Detecting emotional contagion in massive social networks. PloS one **9**(3), e90315 (2014)
11. Ekman, P., Wallace, V.: Unmasking the Face. Malor Book, Cambridge (2003)
12. Izard, C.E.: The Face of Emotion. Appleton-Century-Crofts, New York (1971)
13. Gendron, M., Barrett, L.F.: Reconstructing the past: a century of ideas about emotion in psychology. Emot. Rev. **1**(4), 316–339 (2009)
14. Frijda, N.H.: The Emotions. Cambridge University Press, Cambridge (1986)
15. Lazarus, R.S., Lazarus, R.S.: Emotion and adaptation. Oxford University Press on Demand (1991)
16. Posner, J., Russell, J.A., Peterson, B.S.: The circumplex model of affect: an integrative approach to affective neuroscience, cognitive development, and psychopathology. Dev. Psychopathol. **17**(3), 715–734 (2005)
17. Arnold, M.B.: Emotion and Personality. Columbia University Press, New York (1960)
18. Oatley, K., Johnson-Laird, P.N.: Towards a cognitive theory of emotions. Cogn. Emot. **1**(1), 29–50 (1987)
19. Plutchik, R.: Emotion Theory, Research and Experiences. Academic Press, London (1980)
20. Tomkins, SS.: Affect theory. In: Approaches to emotion, vol. 163, pp. 163–195 (1984)
21. Bann, E.Y., Bryson, J.J.: The conceptualisation of emotion qualia: semantic clustering of emotional tweets. In: Computational Models of Cognitive Processes: Proceedings of the 13th Neural Computation and Psychology Workshop, pp. 249–263. World Scientific (2014)
22. Russell, J.A.: A circumplex model of affect. J. Pers. Soc. Psychol. **39**(6), 1161 (1980)
23. Liu, B.: Sentiment Analysis: Mining Opinions, Sentiments, and Emotions. Cambridge University Press, Cambridge (2015)
24. Medhat, W., Hassan, A., Korashy, H.: Sentiment analysis algorithms and applications: a survey. Ain Shams Eng. J. **5**(4), 1093–1113 (2014)
25. Ravi, K., Ravi, V.: A survey on opinion mining and sentiment analysis: tasks, approaches and applications. Knowl.-Based Syst. **89**, 14–46 (2015)
26. Zucco, C., Calabrese, B., Agapito, G., Guzzi, P.H., Cannataro, M.: Sentiment analysis for mining texts and social networks data: Methods and tools. Wiley Interdisciplinary Reviews: Data Mining and Knowledge Discovery, pp. e1333 (2019)
27. Pang, B., Lee, L., Vaithyanathan, S.: Thumbs up? Sentiment classification using machine learning techniques. In: EMNLP 2002 Proceedings of the ACL-02 Conference on Empirical Methods in Natural Language Processing, pp. 79–86 (2002)
28. Maas, A.L., Daly, R.E., Pham, P.T., Huang, D., Ng, A.Y., Potts, C.: Learning word vectors for sentiment analysis. In: Proceedings of the 49th Annual Meeting of the Association for Computational Linguistics: Human Language Technologies, vol. 1, pp. 142–150. Association for Computational Linguistics (2011)
29. Go, A., Bhayani, R., Huang, L.: Twitter sentiment classification using distant supervision. CS224N Project Report, Stanford, pp. 1–12 (2009)
30. Thelwall, M., Buckley, K., Paltoglou, G., Cai, D., Kappas, A.: Sentiment strength detection in short informal text. J. Am. Soc. Inf. Sci. Technol. **61**(12), 2544–2558 (2010)
31. Mohammad, S., Bravo-Marquez, F., Salameh, M., Kiritchenko, S.: Semeval-2018 task 1: affect in tweets. In: Proceedings of the 12th International Workshop on Semantic Evaluation, pp. 1–17 (2018)

32. Mehrabian, A., Ferris, S.R.: Inference of attitudes from nonverbal communication in two channels. J. Consult. Psychol. **31**(3), 248 (1967)
33. Friesen, W.V., Ekman, P.: Emfacs-7: Emotional facial action coding system. Unpublished manuscript, University of California at San Francisco
34. Lin, C., Xue, G.-R., Zeng, H.-J., Yu, Y.: Using probabilistic latent semantic analysis for personalized web search. In: Zhang, Y., Tanaka, K., Yu, J.X., Wang, S., Li, M. (eds.) APWeb 2005. LNCS, vol. 3399, pp. 707–717. Springer, Heidelberg (2005). https://doi.org/10.1007/978-3-540-31849-1_68
35. Cootes, T.F., Taylor, C.J., Cooper, D.H., Graham, J.: Active shape models-their training and application. Comput. Vis. Image Underst. **61**(1), 38–59 (1995)
36. Ohta, H., Saji, H., Nakatani, H.: Recognition of facial expressions using muscle-based feature models. Syst. Comput. Jpn. **31**(10), 78–88 (2000)
37. Baltrušaitis, T., Robinson, P., Morency, L.-P.: 3D constrained local model for rigid and non-rigid facial tracking. In: 2012 IEEE Conference on Computer Vision and Pattern Recognition, pp. 2610–2617. IEEE (2012)
38. Morency, L.-P., Whitehill, J., Movellan, J.: Generalized adaptive view-based appearance model: Integrated framework for monocular head pose estimation. In: 2008 8th IEEE International Conference on Automatic Face and Gesture Recognition, pp. 1–8. IEEE (2008)
39. Mozziconacci, S.J.L.: Modeling emotion and attitude in speech by means of perceptually based parameter values. User Modeling and User-Adapted Interaction **11**(4), 297–326 (2001)
40. Murray, I.R., Arnott, J.L.: Toward the simulation of emotion in synthetic speech: a review of the literature on human vocal emotion. J. Acoust. Soc. Am. **93**(2), 1097–1108 (1993)
41. Burkhardt, F., Paeschke, A., Rolfes, M., Sendlmeier, W.F., Weiss, B.: A database of German emotional speech. In: Ninth European Conference on Speech Communication and Technology (2005)
42. Haq, S., Jackson, P.J.B., Edge, J.: Audio-visual feature selection and reduction for emotion classification. In: Proceedings of the International Conference on Auditory-Visual Speech Processing (AVSP 2008), Tangalooma, Australia, September 2008
43. Costantini, G., Iaderola, I., Paoloni, A., Todisco, M.: Emovo corpus: an Italian emotional speech database. In: International Conference on Language Resources and Evaluation (LREC 2014), pp. 3501–3504. European Language Resources Association (ELRA) (2014)
44. Zhang, L., Wang, S., Liu, B.: Deep learning for sentiment analysis: a survey. Wiley Interdisciplinary Reviews: Data Mining and Knowledge Discovery, p. e1253 (2018)
45. Li, S., Deng, W.: Deep facial expression recognition: A survey. arXiv preprint arXiv:1804.08348 (2018)
46. dos Santos, C., Gatti, M.: Deep convolutional neural networks for sentiment analysis of short texts. In: Proceedings of COLING 2014, the 25th International Conference on Computational Linguistics: Technical Papers, pp. 69–78 (2014)
47. Kim, Y.: Convolutional neural networks for sentence classification. arXiv preprint arXiv:1408.5882 (2014)
48. Zhou, X., Guo, J., Bie, R.: Deep learning based affective model for speech emotion recognition. In: 2016 International IEEE Conferences on Ubiquitous Intelligence and Computing, Advanced and Trusted Computing, Scalable Computing and Communications, Cloud and Big Data Computing, Internet of People, and Smart World Congress (UIC/ATC/ScalCom/CBDCom/IoP/SmartWorld), pp. 841–846. IEEE (2016)

49. Ruangkanokmas, P., Achalakul, T., Akkarajitsakul, K.: Deep belief networks with feature selection for sentiment classification. In: 2016 7th International Conference on Intelligent Systems, Modelling and Simulation (ISMS), pp. 9–14. IEEE (2016)

50. Jin, Y.: Deep Belief Networks for Sentiment Analysis. Ph.D. thesis, University of New Brunswick (2017)

51. Tai, K.S., Socher, R., Manning, C.D.: Improved semantic representations from tree-structured long short-term memory networks. arXiv preprint arXiv:1503.00075 (2015)

52. Suhara, Y., Xu, Y., Pentland, A.: Deepmood: forecasting depressed mood based on self-reported histories via recurrent neural networks. In: Proceedings of the 26th International Conference on World Wide Web, pp. 715–724. International World Wide Web Conferences Steering Committee (2017)

53. Jain, N., Kumar, S., Kumar, A., Shamsolmoali, P., Zareapoor, M.: Hybrid deep neural networks for face emotion recognition. Pattern Recogn. Lett. **115**, 101–106 (2018)

54. Zhou, D., et al.: Tackling mental health by integrating unobtrusive multimodal sensing. In: AAAI, pp. 1401–1409 (2015)

55. Poria, S., Cambria, E., Howard, N., Huang, G.B., Hussain, A.: Fusing audio, visual and textual clues for sentiment analysis from multimodal content. Neurocomputing **174**, 50–59 (2016)

56. McKeown, G., Valstar, M., Cowie, R., Pantic, M., Schroder, M.: The Semaine database: Annotated multimodal records of emotionally colored conversations between a person and a limited agent. IEEE Trans. Affect. Comput. **3**(1), 5–17 (2011)

57. Douglas-Cowie, E., Cowie, R., Cox, C., Amir, N., Heylen, D.: The sensitive artificial listener: an induction technique for generating emotionally coloured conversation. In: LREC Workshop on Corpora for Research on Emotion and Affect, pp. 1–4. ELRA (2008)

58. Busso, C., et al.: IEMOCAP: interactive emotional dyadic motion capture database. Lang. Resour. Eval. **42**(4), 335 (2008). https://doi.org/10.1007/s10579-008-9076-6

59. Martin, O., Kotsia, I., Macq, B., Pitas, I.: The enterface'05 audio-visual emotion database. In: 22nd International Conference on Data Engineering Workshops (ICDEW 2006), p. 8. IEEE (2006)

Author Index

Printed in the United States
by Baker & Taylor Publisher Services